C000319753

OVERTU

in as

EN
O

We are delighted to have the opportunity to work with Overture Publishing on this series of opera guides and to build on the work ENO did over twenty years ago on the Calder Opera Guide Series. As well as reworking and updating existing titles, Overture and ENO have commissioned new titles for the series and all of the guides will be published to coincide with repertoire being staged by the company at the London Coliseum.

This volume is the third of the Overture Opera Guides to be devoted to Mozart (the earlier volumes were on *Idomeneo* and *Don Giovanni*), and it is issued to mark a new production at ENO of *The Marriage of Figaro*, directed by Fiona Shaw and conducted by Paul Daniel. The cast includes Iain Paterson as Figaro, Devon Guthrie as Susanna, Kate Valentine as the Countess and Roland Wood as the Count.

We hope that these guides will prove an invaluable resource now and for years to come, and that by delving deeper into the history of an opera, the poetry of the libretto and the nuances of the score, readers' understanding and appreciation of the opera and the art form in general will be enhanced.

John Berry
Artistic Director, ENO
October 2011

The publisher John Calder began the Opera Guides series under the editorship of the late Nicholas John in association with English National Opera in 1980. It ran until 1994 and eventually included forty-eight titles, covering fifty-eight operas. The books in the series were intended to be companions to the works that make up the core of the operatic repertory. They contained articles, illustrations, musical examples and a complete libretto and singing translation of each opera in the series, as well as bibliographies and discographies.

The aim of the present relaunched series is to make available again the guides already published in a redesigned format with new illustrations, some newly commissioned articles, updated reference sections and a literal translation of the libretto that will enable the reader to get closer to the meaning of the original. New guides of operas not already covered will be published alongside the redesigned ones from the old series.

Gary Kahn
Series Editor

Sponsors of the Overture Opera Guides

for the 2011/12 Season at ENO

Eric Adler

Frank and Lorna Dunphy

Richard Everall

Ian and Catherine Ferguson

Ralph Wells

Lord and Lady Young

Le nozze di Figaro

Wolfgang Amadeus Mozart

Overture Opera Guides
Series Editor
Gary Kahn

Editorial Consultant
Philip Reed
Head of Publications, ENO

OVERTURE

OVERTURE OPERA GUIDES
in association with

Overture Publishing
an imprint of

ONEWORLD CLASSICS
London House
243–253 Lower Mortlake Road
Richmond
Surrey TW9 2LL
United Kingdom

Articles by John Wells, Basil Deane and Stephen Oliver first published by John Calder (Publishers) Ltd in 1983 © the authors, 1983

Articles by Max Loppert, David Syrus, George Hall and Julian Rushton first published in this volume © the authors, 2011

This *Le nozze di Figaro* Opera Guide first published by Overture Publishing, an imprint of Oneworld Classics Ltd, 2011

© Oneworld Classics Ltd, 2011
All rights reserved

English translation of libretto © Opernführer, Bern

Printed in United Kingdom by TJ International, Padstow, Cornwall

ISBN: 978-1-84749-545-7

All the materials in this volume are reprinted with permission or presumed to be in the public domain. Every effort has been made to ascertain and acknowledge their copyright status, but should there have been any unwitting oversight on our part, we would be happy to rectify the error in subsequent printings.

All rights reserved. No part of this publication may be reproduced, stored in or introduced into a retrieval system, or transmitted, in any form or by any means (electronic, mechanical, photocopying, recording or otherwise), without the prior written permission of the publisher. This book is sold subject to the condition that it shall not be resold, lent, hired out or otherwise circulated without the express prior consent of the publisher.

Contents

List of Illustrations

1. Wolfgang Amadeus Mozart in 1789.
Silverpoint drawing by Doris Stock.

2. Lorenzo Da Ponte as a young man, lithograph from a watercolour (above);
3. Pierre-Augustin Caron de Beaumarchais (below).

4. The Count discovering Chérubin in the chair. One of a series of vignettes by Jacques-Philippe-Joseph de Saint-Quentin from the first authentic edition of the play, published in Kehl in 1785.

5. The Burgtheater in Vienna's Michaelsplatz
at the end of the eighteenth century.

6. Silhouettes of the original 1786 Vienna cast by Hieronymus Löschenkohl. From top left: Stefano Mandini (Count), Luisa Laschi (Countess), Francesco Bussani (Bartolo/Antonio), Maria Mandini (Marcellina).

7. Mozart's autograph score for the beginning of the last scene of the Act Two finale.

ultima

Voi signore che giusto

All: assai

8. Carl Ebert's first production, designed by Hamish Wilson, at the Glyndebourne Festival in 1935. Aulikki Rautawaara as the Countess, Audrey Mildmay as Susanna, Willi Domgraf-Fassbänder as Figaro, Roy Henderson as the Count, Heddle Nash as Basilio, Ronald Stear as Bartolo and Constance Willis as Marcellina (above); 9. Carl Ebert's revised production, designed by Hutchinson Scott, at the Glyndebourne Festival in 1951. Dorothy MacNeil as Cherubino, Lisa Della Casa as the Countess and Genevieve Warner as Susanna (below).

10. Peter Brook's production, designed by Rolf Gérard, at the Royal Opera House in 1950. Sylvia Fisher as the Countess, Geraint Evans as Figaro and Elisabeth Schwarzkopf as Susanna (above);
11. Kiri Te Kanawa as the Countess and Reri Grist as Susanna in John Copley's production, designed by Stefanos Lazaridis, at the Royal Opera House in 1971 (below).

12. Dietrich Fischer-Dieskau as the Count, Graziella Sciutti as Susanna and Evelyn Lear as Cherubino in Gustav Rudolf Sellner's production, designed by Michael Raffaeli, at the Salzburg Festival in 1962 (above);
13. Geraint Evans as Figaro and Reri Grist as Susanna in Günther Rennert's production, designed by Rudolf Heinrich, at the Salzburg Festival in 1970 (below).

14. Jacek Strauch as the Count and John Tomlinson as Figaro in Jonathan Miller's production, designed by Patrick Robertson, at ENO in 1986 (above).
15. Marie McLaughlin as Susanna and Karita Mattila as the Countess in Johannes Schaaf's production, designed by Xenia Hausner, at the Royal Opera House in 1987 (below).

Noted conductors of *Le nozze di Figaro* in the twentieth and twenty-first centuries. From top left: 16. Fritz Busch; 17. Karl Böhm; 18. Charles Mackerras; 19. René Jacobs.

20. Peter Sellars's production, designed by Adrianne Lobel, at the PepsiCo Summerfare in 1988. Jeanne Ommerlé as Susanna and Susan Larson as Cherubino (above); 21. Graham Vick's production, designed by Richard Hudson, at ENO in 1991. Christine Botes as Cherubino, Anthony Michaels-Moore as the Count and Cathryn Pope as Susanna (below).

22. Dieter Dorn's production, designed by Jürgen Rose, at the Bayerische Staatsoper in 1997. Manfred Hemm as Figaro (above);
23. Barrie Kosky's production, designed by Klaus Grünberg, at the Komische Oper, Berlin, in 2005 (below).

24. David McVicar's production, designed by Michael Vale, at the Royal Opera House in 2006 (above); 25. Josse Wieler and Sergio Morabito's production, designed by Barbara Ehnes, at Netherlands Opera in 2006. Gary Magee as the Count and Danielle de Niese as Susanna (below).

26. Claus Guth's production, designed by Christian Schmidt, at the Salzburg Festival in 2006. Patrick Henckens as Basilio, Franz-Josef Selig as Bartolo, Marie McLaughlin as Marcellina, Bo Skovhus as the Count, Uli Kirsch as Cherubino, Anna Netrebko as Susanna, Ildebrando D'Arcangelo as Figaro and Dorothea Röschmann as the Countess (above); 27. Kasper Holten's production, designed by Steffen Aarfing, at the Theater an der Wien in 2007. Anna Bonitatibus as Cherubino and Christopher Maltman as the Count (below).

Living Together, Singing Together

Max Loppert

During his short life, in a manner that now seems incomprehensible to us, Mozart continually encountered obstacles to his progress as a composer of operas, first in his native Salzburg, later in his adopted home city of Vienna. On 1st May 1786 *Le nozze di Figaro* was first performed in the capital, where it did at least gain a respectable success (nine performances in all); but a second *Figaro* production, in 1789, would be required for *Figaro* to win the Viennese acclaim it deserved. And a great deal of time and much tricky negotiation had been needed before Beaumarchais's two-year-old play *La Folle Journée, ou Le Mariage de Figaro* could be made into an opera at all.

This had been Mozart's idea. According to Da Ponte's *Memoirs* it was the composer who at their first meeting, in 1783, had suggested making an opera of Beaumarchais's sequel to his *Barbier de Séville* (1772). A bold proposition: in this play Beaumarchais puts in his characters' mouths stinging criticisms of libertine aristocracy. For this reason, pre-eminent among many, it was banned on completion, in 1781; only three years later did it reach the stage of the Comédie Française in Paris, where it swiftly became one of the greatest triumphs in company history. In Vienna, the Emperor, Joseph II, banned *Le Mariage de Figaro* for performance while granting permission for its publication in both the original language and the vernacular. But Mozart was set on it, and in fact began composing before permission for production was ever granted.

Given the extreme unlikelihood of a commission materializing for an opera made of such volatile material, Baron Raimund von

Wetzlar, a mutual friend of Mozart's and Da Ponte's in whose house the two had first met, in 1783, offered to pay for the libretto and, if Vienna should prove impossible, seek out performance opportunities for the work in London or France. According to the Memoirs – which the reader swiftly learns to take with a large pinch of salt – Da Ponte refused Wetzlar's 'bella generosità': he himself 'proposed to have words and music written secretly and to await a favourable opportunity to show [the opera] to the court theatre directors or to the Emperor himself – the responsibility for the whole undertaking I bravely offered to shoulder myself'. As Da Ponte tells it, soon after the work was completed he succeeded in persuading the reluctant Emperor to let it be performed, and then in quick-wittedly foiling various plots to kill off or in some way mar its eventual production at the Burgtheater.

So finally his and Mozart's opera made it onto this august stage. Shortly before that 1783 first encounter of composer and librettist, the Austrian court theatre had been re-established as a home for Italian comic opera. In 1776 – four years before his mother, Maria Theresa, died – Joseph had taken over its direction himself and immediately disbanded the resident company, thus putting an end to the long-running Viennese tradition of performing Italian and French operas, full-length pantomime ballets, and German plays and Singspiele. In their place came a theatre troupe performing in German, whose activities were extended two years later by the formation of a Singspiel Company (for whom Mozart produced *Die Entführung aus dem Serail*, in 1782). In 1783, however, apparently admitting that his desire to achieve German theatrical dominance at the Burgtheater had not been shared by the public, Joseph reinstated an Italian company alongside the German one. Salieri, already court composer, become its music director and Da Ponte, newly settled in the city, its resident poet.

All this Mozart brought to his father's notice in a letter dated 7th May 1783: 'The Italian opera buffa has started again here and is very popular [...] Our poet now is a certain Abbate Da Ponte', who promises that, after supplying '*per obbligo*' a libretto for Salieri, 'he will write a new libretto for me. But who knows whether he will be able to keep his word – or will want to? [...] If he is in league with Salieri, I shall never get anything out of him. But indeed I should dearly love to show what I can do in an Italian opera.' In the same letter Mozart goes on to lay down what would become, with only small variations, the ground plan for all three of his opera collaborations with Da Ponte: 'The essential thing is that on the whole the story should be really *comic*; and, if possible, [the librettist] ought to introduce *two equally good female parts*, one of these to be *seria*, the other *mezzo carattere*, but both parts equal *in importance and excellence*. The third female character may be entirely *buffa*, and so may all the male ones, if necessary.'

In view of such prescience, it seems yet more amazing that an interval of almost three years intervened between the date of this letter and that of the *Figaro* premiere. But first there was the libretto problem: since nothing was forthcoming from Da Ponte, Mozart began work on *L'oca del Cairo* ('The Cairo Goose'), a new libretto by Varesco, author of *Idomeneo*; two years later he made a start on *Lo sposo deluso* ('The Deluded Bridegroom'), previously set by Domenico Cimarosa. In both cases, after the completion of a few numbers Mozart abandoned the projects. After Da Ponte had agreed to Mozart's Beaumarchais project, the composer appears to have immediately given up *Lo sposo deluso* and taken up *Figaro*. In other words, the right librettist had at last been found and, equally, the right subject matter.

Doubtless, one reason for the attractiveness to Mozart of Beaumarchais's second Figaro play was that he could make his opera a direct sequel to Giovanni Paisiello's operatic adaptation of *Le Barbier de Séville* – this, premiered in St Petersburg in 1780, had been a huge hit in Vienna when given there in summer 1783. The characters were now favourites of the public, and so the new opera would afford Mozart, who liked Paisiello and admired his *Barbiere*, an opportunity of the kind he could never resist, to display the invincible superiority of his musical and theatrical gifts. Then, Beaumarchais's Figaro plays both involve music. In its original form *Le Barbier de Séville* had been intended as an *opéra-comique* (the technical term for a musical drama in which speech and song are mingled), and *Le*

Mariage de Figaro, filled as it is with musical numbers, approached the *opéra-comique* genre more closely than any previous French play. Considerations of this kind would immediately have been appreciated by so naturally theatre-minded an opera-composer as Mozart.

Of his response to the play's notorious political content we have no specific knowledge – not least because unlike in the case of *Idomeneo*, letters charting the *Figaro* birth-process are frustratingly few. One suspects that it held little intrinsic attraction for Mozart. He would have been aware that Beaumarchais's social satire and criticism must require toning down for Vienna. It was surely for reasons deeper than notoriety or the solving of technical problems posed by adaptation that he was drawn to the challenge of a *Figaro* opera.

Three themes running through the play made an especially strong impression on Mozart: of this the music supplies plentiful evidence. One is the plight of women perpetually ill-treated by their menfolk. In the long trial examining the marriage claim against Figaro (which Da Ponte ingeniously reduced to a single short scene), Beaumarchais's Marceline becomes magnificently vocal on the subject: 'You men, worse than ingrates, who destroy through contempt the playthings of your passions – your victims! – it is you who ought to be punished for the mistakes of our youth!'

Such uncomfortable outbursts Da Ponte may have excised (and the operatic Dr Bartolo submits far more quietly to marriage than his Beaumarchais counterpart). But what remains carries the underlying message clearly enough: the mighty comic engines of *Le nozze di Figaro* are constantly fuelled by stratagems – many of them devised, admittedly, by Figaro – for gaining women their freedom, however temporary, from the unjust or improper actions of men. In the long finale of Act Two, widely held to be the greatest single example of ensemble writing in all opera, Mozart's powers of dramatization are at full stretch: his immeasurably brilliant exploration for dramatic purposes of sonata-form principles, command of in-depth psychological analysis through melody, and comprehension of the human voice in all manner of combination and contrast – of this last the finale's graded expansion from three participants through four to seven, spatially divided (two groups of three on either side of the

Count), provides perhaps the matchless demonstration. Everything fuses to develop this theme of stratagem and strategy to the point of comic combustion.

Another theme is female alliance, often, not always, as a direct response to men's unjust or improper actions. In the opera, unlike the play, Figaro and the Count are never alone together: Da Ponte left their battles of wills and wits to be exemplified by confrontations during the ensemble scenes of Acts Two and Three. Indeed, until the fifth scene of the opera's fourth act, in which Figaro assembles a handful of men (Bartolo, Basilio, a few workmen) to witness Susanna's supposed forthcoming infidelity, no scene displays any purely male grouping. Of women together, on the other hand, the treatment is wonderfully substantial and expressive. We see Susanna alone with Marcellina once, and – central to the opera's endlessly vital, full-hearted perception of women – Susanna alone with the Countess thrice: first in Act Two; then in Act Three, while the latter dictates the letter by means of which the Count will be drawn to the assignation 'under the pines' that the two have prepared for him; and finally in Act Four, just before their garden venture in exchanged costumes.

The simplest of musical devices, that of two voices echoing each other's melodic phrases, is employed to characterize two of these meetings, to widely differing ends. In the Act One duet for Susanna and Marcellina, 'Via resti servita' ('After you'), the notes sung are exactly the same much of the time, taken up each in turn with spitfire vivacity, but the words are different: Marcellina's every phrase of mock deference is trumped by Susanna's ripostes, and the result is a perfect comic essay-in-miniature on women at war in polite society. (This demonstration in purely vocal terms of apparently irreconcilable differences provides the backdrop, as Mozart the long-range dramatic psychologist meant it to, for the sublimely concordant coda to the Act Three sextet, 'Riconosci in questo amplesso / una madre, amato figlio' ('Dearest son, in this embrace / recognize your mother') in which Susanna's voice with overflowing happiness rises atop then sinks below Marcellina's to speak volumes about reconciliation achieved. From this moment Marcellina is one of Susanna's staunchest allies.) In the Act Three Letter Scene, in contrast, echo-repetition is used to touch in the feelings of affectionate trust and, indeed, emotional equality that mistress and maidservant are capable of showing each other while developing their battle plan. The first time round the Countess states the melody and Susanna repeats it, the second Susanna states what has been dictated to her and the Countess varies her repetitions, then both vary and embellish, until at the close the two come together in a blissful chain of thirds and sixths.

The third theme of the play to which Mozart appears particularly responsive – it is this, I believe, perhaps more than any other aspect of the opera, that places it among the central, essential, eternally self-renewing works of western art – is the depiction of various types of love-relationship within the context of normal life. Like few other operas – *Die Meistersinger von Nürnberg* and *Falstaff* come to mind – *Le nozze di Figaro* draws its dramatic incident out of a created 'real world', an environment peopled with recognizable, three-dimensional types of different station in close proximity. On the Count's estate at Aguas Frescas, work gets done, and in spite of passing intrigue, misunderstanding and friction, people carry on co-existing. For all the gloriously farcical improbabilities that occur during this particular 'mad day', it is not the comedy alone that makes *Le nozze di Figaro* a never-ending source of pleasure, emotional nourishment, and instruction on how to live with one's fellow human beings. Vertical family relationships are few – while Figaro's previously unknown parents make themselves known during the opera, the revelation is a comic plot-hinge rather than a component of any dramatization of child-parent relationships; and the Countess's illegitimate child, fruit of a brief sexual relationship with Cherubino and subject of *L'Autre Tartuffe, ou La Mère coupable* of 1792, Beaumarchais's third Figaro play, has yet to be conceived.

Yet the impression one gains during the opera is of several generations and types of family cohabiting in or else visiting a particular household, with different levels of conflict, truce and concord stratified throughout, and with traditional practices and ceremonials honoured at crucial places. Pregnant though it may be with plot-advancement points, and regularly punctuated by the Count's fretful mutterings, the culmination of the third act is the operatic medium's most complete and rounded dramatization of weddings as ordinary people often experience them in ordinary life: smiles, tears, moments of discomfort and dissatisfaction, and at some point everyone merrily dancing.

All this attests to the psychologically acute character-observation that the opera demonstrates: informed by all the vivacity and ingenuity of Beaumarchais's play (if not its 'political' energy), and with the immeasurable enrichment of Mozart's music. At its heart are the four types of love-involvement, with sexual attraction an inevitable and fascinatingly variable ingredient, which gives the character-observation its peculiar combination of good humour, depth and poignancy. At one extreme of age (and libido) there is Cherubino, just past puberty. Mozart's and Da Ponte's adherence to theatrical tradition in having the young aristocrat played *en travesti* – a boy (impersonated by a woman) who is then required to dress up as a girl – releases in the character a pan-sexual allure that permits adolescents of any and every sexual persuasion (and age) to identify with him; no knowledge of *La Mère coupable* is necessary to reach the end of the opera suspecting that Cherubino and Barbarina will not long remain an 'item'. At the other extreme are Bartolo and Marcellina, every flicker extinguished of the 'antico amor' that long ago brought Figaro into being: no singing together here! Having begun the opera both determined, for entirely opposite reasons, that Marcellina should win both her case and Figaro, they end it in a state of marital truce.

Between these come the Figaro-Susanna and Count-Countess couples: and it is here that Mozart's comprehension of the human voice in combination and contrast is most fully revealed. Not solely in their arias do the four make this manifest: it is on their method and manner of singing together – when this occurs and in what context – that Mozart focuses his exploration and development of these two relationships. The nub of the opera's opening number is Susanna's teaching Figaro – who at the start is busily measuring out room-lengths – to sing her tune, which at bar 49 he begins to do. This forms the psychological background to their second number together, at the opposite end of the opera, in the Act Four finale. Here

Figaro, having finally seen through Susanna-in-Countess-disguise, pretends to make advances to the *finta Contessa*, upsetting Susanna thoroughly; then in 'Pace, pace, mio dolce tesoro' ('Now peace, my dearest treasure') he reassures her that all along he recognized 'the voice I love', and at bar 11 she takes up *his* tune while his lower-line harmonization provides the thirds and sixths that, along with the lovingly rocking $\frac{6}{8}$ rhythm, make us confident that their partnership is an equal one, sturdy and of long-lasting substance.

In sharp contrast, the only episode showing the Count and Countess vocally alone together, 'Esci omai, garzon malnato' ('Now out you come, you imp of Satan') in Act Two, pictures them seriously in conflict, revealing through the soprano's and baritone's varieties and contrasts of *vocalità* some of the character traits that have set them apart – his easily provoked rage, puffed-up sense of honour, and baseless mistrust of his wife, her innate dignity and grace even *in extremis*. In the opera's emotional climax, just before the final bars of the final act, their voices appear to make peace with each other: the Count's simple four-bar plea, 'Contessa, perdono' ('My Countess, forgive me'), followed by the Countess's six-bar reply. Yet in this passage of sublime simplicity there is also profound pathos, which emanates as much from the character differences that these ten bars underline as from their calming sentiments. The way her voice 'tops' his, the way her phrases prove at once more supple, more rounded and (by two bars) more expansive than his – these small details speak, again, volumes about the course their marriage is likely to take. The termination of the 'folle giornata' is a many-voiced bustle of D major merriment, which is heard to be, in both key and rhythmic pattern, a blood relative of the D major overture. But just beneath this exhilarating surface, some poignant facts of 'real life' – the servants' marriage will surely last, the masters' probably not – remain for our contemplation: not, perhaps, while the mood of closing elation is still strong, but once it has begun to die down.

A Society Marriage

John Wells

According to Beaumarchais, the author of the original play, *Le Mariage de Figaro* was written at the request of that pillar of the Ancien Régime, the Prince de Conti, Commander-in-Chief of the Army under Louis XV. According to Napoleon, it was part of the mechanism of the Revolution, a central cog already beginning to turn as early as six o'clock in the evening of Tuesday 27th April 1784, when the play received its first public performance in Paris at the Comédie Française.

Both statements are probably true, and for anyone interested in the mysterious interaction between art and politics, it would be hard to find a more fascinating story: Beaumarchais, watchmaker to Madame de Pompadour, secret agent to Louis XVI, creating a piece of dramatic machinery credited with the destruction of the society that commissioned it, only to be turned, by Mozart and Da Ponte, into a work of art in which we recognize the most perfect flowering of the civilization it is alleged to have destroyed.

Pierre-Auguste Caron de Beaumarchais had been born plain Caron in 1732, the son of a watchmaker in the rue St Denis. His first revolutionary act, at the age of twenty-one, was to invent a new kind of escapement, enabling him to make a watch that was not only accurate to the second, but also small enough to fit inside a ring, and this he presented to Madame de Pompadour. The court watchmaker, Lepaute, claimed that he had invented it first, but Caron protested to the Academy of Sciences, won his case, and took over Lepaute's Royal Patent.

He strengthened his position at Versailles by marrying an influential but, as he discovered on her death a year later, penniless widow, from whose estate in the country however he took the title de Beaumarchais, adopting the very suitable motto 'Ma Vie est un Combat'. By the age of twenty-seven he had further established himself with characteristic versatility as music master to the daughters of Louis XV, and taught them his favourite instrument, the harp. From this followed various well-paid court appointments, including the administration of hunting rights, which required him to spend a considerable amount of time in the law courts, passing judgment on poaching offences. He also formed lucrative associations with some of the leading financiers of the day.

In 1764 he made a journey to Madrid, combining the discreet advancement of French business interests in the newly-acquired Spanish colony of Louisiana with the official purpose of his visit, which was to straighten out a breach of promise case between his elder sister, Lisette, who was then thirty-nine, and a Spanish journalist called Clavijo. Beaumarchais's own account of the two men's meeting, his arriving incognito, fascinating his adversary with a tale of faithless love, and then, in a final *coup de théâtre,* revealing himself as the brother of the abandoned woman, was subsequently to provide Goethe with the plot of his drama *Clavigo*.

Beaumarchais's own first excursion into the theatre, *Eugénie,* was written in 1767, when he was thirty-five. It was in the style of uplifting middle-class realism advocated by Diderot, known as the *drame bourgeois,* and was given a mixed reception. His second, *Les Deux Amis, ou le Négociant de Lyon,* was written three years later and failed entirely. But he had also been writing comedy, in the form of what were called *parades*: coarse, knockabout sketches, performed privately, 'in the flickering shadows of the drawing-room', popular in fashionable society, but based on the rough street-theatre of the Paris Fairs. He had also seen similar shows in Madrid, known as *entreméses,* which incorporated the Barber as a stock comic character.

Life too was providing him with some rich material. He had married again, this time to a widow with money, who had died two years later. He had also come into an inheritance, left to him by one of his financiers, Pâris-Duvernay, which he successfully defended against rival claimants. In 1773, at the age of forty-one, he became involved in a farcical quarrel over a certain Mlle Ménard, which was to leave him bankrupt, in disgrace, but with a lasting and genuine hatred of hereditary privilege, and also, by a skilful use of journalism and stage management, with the public reputation of a revolutionary hero struggling against oppression.

His opponent was the Duc de Chaulnes, a grotesquely fat and violently irascible man who went about with a monkey on a chain. Until then, he and Beaumarchais had been the best of friends: now Chaulnes threatened to kill him, dragged him from the bench where he was trying a poaching case, ripped the wigs from the heads of anyone who tried to interfere, snatched a pen out of Beaumarchais's hand and threw it out of the window, scratched his face and stabbed his servant through the hand with a fork. As a result they were both imprisoned.

Hearing that the magistrate was to be a notoriously corrupt individual by the name of Goëzman, Beaumarchais sent his wife a jewelled watch and a hundred louis to ease the wheels of justice. Madame Goëzman accepted the present, and asked for a further fifteen louis for the clerk. How much Chaulnes gave her is not on record, but Beaumarchais lost the case and was ordered to pay costs and a crushing fine which reduced him to penury. Madame Goëzman, very decently, returned the hundred louis and the watch, but kept the fifteen louis she had demanded for the clerk. Having made it his motto that life was a battle, Beaumarchais counter-attacked. Without a penny to his name and his seventy-five-year-old father turned out into the street, he launched a series of pamphlets, the *Memorials against Goëzman*, admitting the entire truth and demanding the return of his fifteen louis. Goëzman was dismissed, Beaumarchais publicly disgraced and deprived of his rights as a citizen.

Mysteriously, Louis XVI retained his services as a secret agent, and during his ensuing exile in London Beaumarchais continued to work for Versailles, rooting out and suppressing the publishers of anti-royalist French pamphlets. He also, lest farce be forgotten entirely, lent assistance to another French agent, the Chevalier d'Éon, a transvestite of vigorously heterosexual leanings who was to be seen lifting his dress in the drawing rooms of fashionable London society to expose his battle scars, and was believed by some to be the father of George IV. Beaumarchais negotiated a pension for him from the King of France with which he bought a wardrobe of expensive dresses for the Chevalier's return to Versailles; there was general disappointment when he arrived there dressed as a dragoon, only reverting to a frock for his second day at court.

Before embarking on his next adventurous career, running guns to General Washington, which also cost him a fortune since the American Revolutionaries presumably saw no cause to pay once French 'military advisers' became official allies, Beaumarchais returned to France in 1775 for the first performance of *Le Barbier de Séville*. It opened on 23 February and was booed off by the first-night audience.

'Seeing the enemy relentless,' he writes in his mock-pompous defence of the play in a preface to the first edition, 'the pit restless, rough and roaring aloud like the waves of the sea, and all too well aware that grumbling thunder of that kind can herald storms that have brought about the wreck of more than one proud enterprise, I fell to thinking that many plays in five acts (like my own), although excellently made in every particular (like my own), would not have foundered lock, stock and barrel (like my own), if the author had taken a bold decision (like my own). *The God of the Cabal is angry!* I cried aloud to the actors: *Children! We needs must make some sacrifice*. Then, giving the devil his due and ripping my manuscript apart: *God of the hissers, booers and disturbers of the peace,* I roared, *Must you have blood? Then take Act Four and may your fury be appeased!*' After a weekend of cutting and re-staging the show reopened and was immediately a success. 'Poor Figaro, who had been unmercifully thrashed to the monotonous chanting of the Cabal, and almost buried on Friday [...] rose again on Sunday with a vigour that the rigours of a long Lent and the fatigue of twenty-seven public performances have not yet sapped. But who knows how long it can go on? Not more than five or six hundred years at the very most, I should have said, in a country as fickle and unpredictable as France!'

Whether or not Beaumarchais realized that he had written a play that would survive his own century, he must have recognized that in his Andalusian barber he, and the liberal-minded majority of the theatre-going public, had found a mouthpiece. Frédéric Grendel[1] has argued very plausibly that Figaro *was* Beaumarchais, '*Fils* – pronounced in the eighteenth century *Fi* – Caron', and that all the autobiographical details, particularly during the long monologue in the original *Le Mariage de Figaro,* tally exactly with the events in the author's life. Certainly the figure of the barber with his razor resting against the Count's Adam's apple is a powerful image of the vigorous middle class confronting hereditary privilege.

It is in the same preface to *Le Barbier de Séville* that Beaumarchais imagines what might happen after the curtain comes down: Bartholo and Figaro are still arguing about money, and begin hitting each other. In the course of the brawl that follows, the old doctor is punching Figaro's head when he sees the mark of a hot spatula and stops to cry out in delight: Figaro is his long-lost son, stolen away by gypsies. Marceline is his mother. 'What an end to the play! What an Act Six! Better than any tragedy at the Théâtre Français! But enough of that...'

This is the story, Beaumarchais claims in his preface to *Le Mariage de Figaro*, that the Prince de Conti challenged him to make into a sequel. What the public, and what Beaumarchais wanted, was more Figaro. The main plot, he explains in the second preface, is extremely simple: 'a Spanish grandee, in love with a girl he intends to seduce, and her efforts, those of her future husband and the grandee's wife to frustrate him in a design that his position in society, his wealth and his dissolute character make him entirely capable of accomplishing.'

By the time Mozart and Da Ponte began work on the opera in Vienna in 1785, the play had already caused an uproar in Paris, and Joseph II, the Austrian Emperor, had banned a version that was to have been performed there. Da Ponte therefore set about reducing its overtly political content to a minimum, cutting a great deal of Figaro's verbal skirmishing with the Count, and the whole of his

---

1 Frédéric Grendel, *Beaumarchais, The Man Who Was Figaro*, trans. Roger Graves (London: Macdonald and Jane's, 1977).

long tirade against privilege as he waits under the chestnut trees – Da Ponte transformed them into pine trees, perhaps in some fit of Italianate yearning for the North – for the feudal lord he believes is about to plunder his 'property' in the person of Suzanne. Marceline's speech in defence of women's rights, on the other hand, which follows her reconciliation with Figaro and the doctor, and which had been suppressed in Paris by the actors themselves, was partially retained by Da Ponte in Marcellina's aria in Act Four, though it is not always performed.

But even with Figaro's closing couplet of the *vaudeville,* the song and dance that brings the stage play to an end, in which he compares the mortality of kings to the immortal glory awaiting Voltaire, it is difficult to imagine the play creating more than a frisson of drawing-room egalitarianism in the extravagantly dressed stars of Parisian high society who crammed the new auditorium of the Comédie Française – 'that mine of white icing sugar' – for the five hours of cheering and rapturous applause that marked the first performance. The play did literally bring about the death of three enthusiastic theatregoers, crushed by the crowd of five thousand that besieged the theatre from eight o'clock in the morning and poured in when the gates were opened at twelve noon, six hours before the curtain was due to rise. According to one account, their dead bodies were held upright by the weight of numbers, and appeared to be listening to the play. But it was predominantly an aristocratic audience, three hundred of whom thought it was the greatest privilege to be allowed to eat a picnic in the actors' dressing rooms. The artistic event of the century, perhaps, but not, on the face of it, a great political turning point.

The answer to the riddle is to be found in the mainspring of the plot. The Count, having renounced the *droit de seigneur*, his absolute power over his subjects, is trying illicitly to re-establish it. Louis XVI, vacillating over the liberal reforms that Beaumarchais believed would lead to a constitutional monarchy, behaved in exactly the same way. When Beaumarchais gave him the manuscript to read in 1782, he said it would be necessary to demolish the Bastille before the play could be performed in public without embarrassing the government. Combative as ever, Beaumarchais organized a series of private readings that became the rage of Paris, and the King in response to pressure at court gave his permission for a private performance at Versailles in the summer of 1783. Beaumarchais rehearsed it for four weeks, and three hours before the curtain was to go up the King cancelled it. Rage and despair on the part of the audience, wild talk of tyranny and oppression.

By September of the same year the King had changed his mind again, and allowed a single performance at Grennevilliers, the country house of the Comte de Vandreuil. Marie Antoinette was to have been present, but at the last minute sent apologies and said she was unwell. Gaining fresh momentum from this success, the publicity campaign continued. Beaumarchais called a semi-public meeting with the six official censors, arguing through the play line by line, delighting privileged spectators with his wit and skilfully incorporating their more amusing suggestions in the text: Madame de Matignon was credited with inventing the colour of Chérubin's ribbon. Permission was granted, and after a two-year build-up, the comedy scored what was probably the most spectacular success of any opening night in history.

A few days later, as if that triumph was not enough, Beaumarchais tested the weakness of the government to even more excruciatingly absurd limits. Irritated by an attack from Suard, the Chief of Police, he said that when he had done battle with lions and tigers he couldn't be bothered with repulsive little insects that only dared to bite under cover of darkness. Not wishing to be listed among the big cats vanquished by the lion-tamer, Louis XVI, after customary hesitation, scribbled an order for his arrest on the seven of spades during a game of cards, and Beaumarchais was imprisoned. Instead of the Bastille, reserved for respectable political opponents, he was confined in Saint-Lazare, a leper hospital and the gaol for prostitutes and petty thieves.

A gigantic sum was raised by his friends for bail, intercession was made at Versailles, and the King wrote an order for his immediate release. Beaumarchais ignored it. He would not leave the prison until he had an assurance that the entire Cabinet would attend *Le Mariage de Figaro* 'as a gesture of respect for the author'. Incredibly, they did so, rising to their feet at the end of the performance and applauding him. By way of making additional amends, the King also organized a gala performance of *Le Barbier de Séville* at Versailles, with Marie Antoinette playing Rosine.

Many of those who metaphorically lost their heads at the first night of *Le Mariage de Figaro* died on the guillotine. Beaumarchais was exiled, once again for gun-running, and remained abroad until 1796, when he returned, still clinging to his title, as Citizen Caron de Beaumarchais, describing it as his *nom de guerre*. He had continued to promote extravagant schemes, including a complete edition of the works of Voltaire with lottery prizes for those lucky enough to buy certain numbered copies and a gigantic monument to Liberty on the site now occupied by the Eiffel Tower. At the height of the Terror he had been working on the third and last of the Figaro plays, *La Mère coupable* (*A Mother's Guilt*): this time it is set in the present. Aguas Frescas, the Almavivas' estate, has been sold up; the Count, now plain Monsieur Almaviva, is living in Paris. The comedy is over, and the pigeons have come home to roost. Chérubin, having given the Countess an illegitimate child, has died in despair on the battlefield, Almaviva has brought his daughter by another woman to live in the house as his ward, their only legitimate child has been shot dead in a duel, and the family is being preyed upon by a villainous Irish adventurer, Captain Bégearss, inevitably based on yet another personal enemy of Beaumarchais, a lawyer called Bergasse. It is left to Figaro and Suzanne, now grown old in service, to unmask and expel the interloper.

The play, which had met with a lukewarm reception before his exile, was revived with great success on his return, and Napoleon claimed that it was his favourite work. After months spent studying the possibilities of aviation, a chance, he felt, that had been missed and 'that could have changed the face of the earth more radically than the invention of the compass', Beaumarchais died in his sleep, probably of apoplexy, in the spring of 1799. His energy and fighting spirit survive in his greatest work, *Le Mariage de Figaro*: still sufficiently alarming to authority, for all the ambiguity of its political origins, to have been banned at the Comédie Française throughout the German Occupation.

A Musical Commentary

Basil Deane

'Dramma per musica' – drama through music: the oldest, and still the best, definition of opera. And the character of any opera will be determined by the manner in which the librettist and composer resolve the inherent tension between these two elements. For tension there must be. There are many types of drama; but all involve individuals in specific circumstances interacting with and reacting to outside events, in a recognizably human timescale. Music is an unspecific art, and it functions within its own structures and its own timescale. It must be integrated with the drama in a way that illuminates the characters and articulates the action, without losing its unique expressive power. The history of opera is the history of attempted solutions to this problem.

By the eighteenth century Italian opera had assumed two fairly stylized forms. *Opera seria* dealt with important personages participating in grand historical or mythological events. These individuals expressed themselves in a series of arias projecting their current emotional state. And here arises at its most acute the problem of dramatic and musical reconciliation. An unbroken succession of soliloquies is not after all the customary mode of human communication. The problem is compounded by the structure of the aria. It is in ternary, or ABA, form. The return of the first section brings the music back to the home key and allows the singer to embellish the original melody. However desirable musically, in terms of advancing the action this procedure is inherently undramatic since the composer also returns to the original text. The return of the first section, necessary for musical reasons, is, in terms of advancing the action, inherently undramatic. The best composers were of course aware of the difficulty, and the approach by a composer such as Handel to the aria is of the greatest interest. But in the hands of lesser figures *opera seria* became a series of staged concert arias, in which the dramatic structure was irrelevant or virtually absent.

The alternative form, *opera buffa,* was not so stereotyped. In the comic operas of Cimarosa and Paisiello, for example, the characters, drawn from less exalted stations, often had a liveliness and a naturalness missing in *opera seria*. Musical numbers were shorter, and simple ensembles played a more prominent part. The action moved forward more rapidly. But the fairly restricted musical idioms allowed for little depth of character portrayal. Nevertheless it was this tradition which, however modestly, provided the foundation for Mozart's great *opera buffa*.

Beaumarchais's play, it is well recognized, is in several senses revolutionary. So, too, in dramatic terms, is Da Ponte's libretto. It stands head and shoulders above all the earlier *opera buffa* librettos by virtue of its length, its combination of clarity and complexity, its consistency, its momentum. But perhaps the most revolutionary thing about it is its use of ensembles. Of its twenty-eight numbers, only half are for solo voice. Such a concentration on ensembles was unprecedented in eighteenth-century opera. It brought a new dramatic and psychological realism to the medium. Instead of taking characters and their emotions at their own word, so to speak, audiences could now see and evaluate them in a variety of social contexts. This above all was the great opportunity that Da Ponte's libretto offered to Mozart – the opportunity of presenting fully-rounded characters in a range of evolving situations. The composer understood this, and by musical genius transformed the already brilliant concept of Da Ponte into one of the great masterpieces of dramatic art.

He was, in compositional terms, extremely well equipped to do so. The classical style reached maturity in the 1780s. The symphony, concerto and sonata offered flexible, coherent forms, based on the integration of contrasting musical ideas, both small- and large-scale. The composition of the orchestra became standardized and the combination of strings, wind and percussion offered a wide potential of textures and instrumental colours. By the time he came to write *Figaro* Mozart was already a master of this new, exciting language; indeed he himself had already made a major contribution to its rapid and continuing evolution. The Overture is itself a fine illustration of his superb accomplishment as an instrumental composer. It is based on three main themes [1, 2, 3].[1] All his fingerprints are manifest; brilliant tuttis, singing melodies, imaginative orchestration, rhythmic drive, subtly varied harmonies. Its powerful drive and its elegance and carefully calculated detail belie the haste in which it was written, a matter of hours before the first performance.

The Overture ends, the curtain rises, and Figaro, Count Almaviva's valet and Susanna, Countess Almaviva's maid, are together, Figaro measuring the room they have been allocated after their marriage and Susanna trying on her wedding hat. The orchestral introduction epitomizes Mozart's approach to musical characterization. The passage contains two contrasting themes, one robust, the other insinuating [4, 5]. In the duet Figaro is associated with the first, Susanna with the second. Susanna is gently insistent that she should have Figaro's undivided attention, and he eventually abandons his measurements, and his theme, joining her in harmonious tenths. Not only are the personalities of the two protagonists outlined; Susanna's capacity for leading her betrothed is established as is also the warmth in their relationship.

The following duet tells us more about them. Figaro has taken the Count's gift of this convenient room at face value; Susanna is much more attuned to her employer's real motives. This time they both use a variant of the same theme [6]. But the tone of Susanna's ironical answer to Figaro is deliciously established by a pre-emptive switch to the minor key. Figaro is not stupid. He takes Susanna's point, and again the duet ends in unity.

Up until now, Susanna has made the running. Now Figaro, seeing the situation clearly for the first time, asserts himself. Mozart chooses the framework of a courtly minuet, no doubt with the Count in mind [7]. But as the music progresses, the symbolic sounds of the horns,

1 Numbers in square brackets refer to the Thematic Guide on pp. 75–82 [Ed.].

doubled by pizzicato strings, and the sudden leaps in the vocal part, as well as the stabbing accents, convey Figaro's anger, which breaks the conventional surface in the *Presto* outburst [8]. Figaro aroused is to be reckoned with.

Bartolo, a doctor, and Marcellina, the housekeeper, now arrive. Middle-aged and worldly, they form a contrast to the young lovers. Here for the first time in the opera Mozart draws on the resources of *opera seria*. Among the categories of aria employed in *opera seria* was the 'rage' aria. Bartolo gives vent to his delight at the prospect of revenge on Figaro in a parodied example of the type, full of unison passages, accompanied by the pomp of horns, trumpets and drums [9]. The quick 'patter' passage in the middle belongs however to the *buffa* world [10].

The women's relationship is no less antagonistic, but socially concealed. In the following duet an exchange of compliments turns quickly into one of insults, in which Susanna has all the natural advantages. The exchange [11] is repeated, and here occurs an example of the conflict between musical and dramatic exigencies. Dramatically the repetition of the text is most implausible; since Marcellina has been deeply insulted and bested, she is very unlikely to go through the same situation again. But, although Mozart describes this number (as he did the earlier ones) as a duettino, to end after the first exchange would have been musically too sudden. So here, as in other similar situations, the resolution in stage terms depends ultimately on the skill of the director and the singers.

Cherubino, the Count's page, now enters. In Beaumarchais's time the emotional development and sexual education of adolescents was of fashionable interest in French aristocratic circles. Cherubino, the Countess's page, is in the tradition. He is still in the initial stages of discovery and self-awareness, in love with love. His longings are diffuse, his affections transferable. His aria, with its breathless phrases, its palpitating accompaniment, its hesitant chromaticisms, evokes the excitement of his emotions [12].

So far the Count has been an unseen but potentially threatening influence on events. With his appearance the action quickens. Cherubino, fearful of his wrath, hides. The Count resumes his attempted seduction of Susanna, but, on the arrival of Basilio, the music teacher, he too conceals himself. The stage is set for a classic piece of situation comedy. Basilio's insinuations about the page's relationship with the Countess bring the infuriated husband out of hiding. The terzetto that follows provides Mozart with his first opportunity in the opera for building a large-scale musical structure, and dramatic and musical content are mutually dependent. The emotions of the three characters are embodied in the opening material: the Count's rage, momentarily contained, then given full vent [13]; Basilio's silky obsequiousness [14a]; Susanna's apprehension [14b]. These three elements provide much of the subsequent musical material. When the music moves from B flat to its second key of F, there is a momentary lull as both men hasten to support Susanna when she pretends to faint. But her perception of the danger of revealing Cherubino, and her quick reaction, hurry the action and the music onward. Basilio smoothly reintroduces the subject of the page again, and, as the Count resumes his initial threats, so too the opening material returns, now varied, re-ordered and expanded to encompass the discovery of Cherubino. Perfectly illustrative of the developing action, the terzetto, 220 bars long, is in fact a fully-fledged movement in sonata form.

The chorus of peasants [15], led by Figaro, praising the Count, has in itself a charming folk-like simplicity. In the context of Figaro's new attitude to his master, and of the immediately preceding events, its dramatic purport is, of course, ironical.

To begin an *opera buffa* with a duet is in itself unusual; to end an act with a solo is more so. Convention dictated that this was the place for an ensemble. But no exit could be more effective than that of Cherubino, departing reluctantly for the wars. Figaro's aria became an instant 'hit' when the opera was performed in Prague, and it has remained one ever since. As so often, a straightforward exterior conceals great art. Those who know the aria well (and who does not?) should observe the detail of the orchestral accompaniment [16]; the contrasting textures; the woodwind and string embellishments; the sparing use of trumpets and drums until Cherubino sets out for victory and glory in a blaze of fanfares [17].

One principal figure has still to be introduced: the Countess. She has a dignity and restraint appropriate to her position, yet she is also a loving wife, deeply wounded by her husband's behaviour. A *seria* rather than a *buffa* character, she makes her entrance fittingly at the beginning of Act Two with a solo number, in which she implores the gods to revive her husband's love. Mozart eschews the fully-fledged aria. Instead he writes a cavatina – a single section composition in which she retains her outward poise; the melodic line is chaste and tender, and moves above a simple but firm bass line [18]. But her inner agitation is conveyed by the gently throbbing accompaniment figure, with its poignant chromatic inflections. This textural combination is not uncommon in Mozart's mature slow movements, as, for example, in the String Quartet in E flat major K428. Nowhere is it more dramatically effective than here. The characterization is enhanced by the first use in the opera of a pair of clarinets as obbligato instruments, moving in melting euphony.

In the second scene of the Act, which takes place in recitative, Figaro expounds to the two women his plot to confuse and ensnare the Count by arousing the latter's suspicions about his wife's fidelity. The Countess, understandably, is hesitant; but she is won over by the lovers, and Figaro reaffirms his intention of making the Count dance to his tune. Cherubino, who has contrived to delay his departure, joins the women, and is easily persuaded to sing the song he has composed for the Countess [19]. Its blend of youthful hope and uncertainty is irresistible. In preparation for the intrigue against the Count, Susanna makes Cherubino try on a dress, and sings a cheerful, busy aria while she fits him out [20].[2] The scene projects a subtle blend of comedy and underlying eroticism, and the Countess's amusement is tinged with anxiety. And indeed, the Count's arrival outside the locked door changes the atmosphere from laughter to fear.

Susanna has left. Cherubino, half undressed, hides in the dressing room. The Count, entering the room, demands to know who

2 Mozart replaced this aria with 'Un moto di gioia' ('I feel stirrings of joy') K579 for the 1789 revival of the opera in Vienna, when Adriana Ferraresi, Lorenzo Da Ponte's mistress, sang Susanna. See Libretto, p. 160 and Thematic Guide music example [22], p. 77 [Ed.].

is in there. The Countess, terrified, says it is Susanna. The Count demands proof. Meanwhile Susanna slips back in, and unobserved, witnesses the drama. In this terzetto [21] Mozart again uses sonata form. But this time the tension is unrelieved. The music maintains its impetus, with the Count becoming increasingly enraged, and the two women more and more fearful. The sudden shifts from *p* to *f* serve to intensify the violence of the Count's emotions. When the Count storms out, taking his reluctant wife with him, Susanna and Cherubino have a quick whispered exchange before the page escapes by jumping from the window, and Susanna takes his place [24]. The Count, armed with tools to break down the door, returns with the Countess who, believing that all is lost, confesses that the person in the dressing room is Cherubino.

Now begins what is surely one of Mozart's most monumental achievements: the finale to Act Two. In its scale, its complexity and its integration of dramatic and musical meaning, it is without precedent and has never been surpassed. The range of the whole edifice may best be displayed in tabular form:

Sc. 8	Count & Countess Duet	E flat major	*Allegro*	125 bars [26]
Sc. 9	Susanna enters Terzet	B flat major	*Molto andante-allegro*	201 bars [27]
Sc. 10	Figaro enters Quartet	G major	*Allegro*	69 bars [28]
		C major	*Andante*	68 bars [29]
Sc. 11	Antonio enters Quintet	F	*Allegro molto*	137 bars
		B flat major	*Andante*	[30]
Sc. 12	Marcellina, Bartolo & Basilio enter Septet	E flat major	*Allegro assai più allegro*	243 bars [31]

The musical structure has a rock-like solidity, an unbroken continuity and a totally symphonic breadth. It begins and ends with two massive sections in E flat major. In between it moves, as usual, first to the dominant key (B flat major), then it returns by a series of logical steps from G major to the home key. The sections are contrasted in tempo and metre, each one containing its own thematic material. All are related strictly to the evolution of the dramatic situation, as more detailed consideration will show.

The first scene is dominated by the Count. His rage increases as the Countess attempts to explain why he will find Cherubino in a state of undress. He denounces the Countess in biting accents and, despite her pleadings, is on the point of breaking down the door, when it opens, and out comes, not the page, but Susanna [27]. The musical change is magical. To the most innocent of minuet rhythms, played by strings alone, Susanna expresses her bewilderment at all the fuss. For different reasons, both Count and Countess are momentarily stunned. But they recover, and as they do the music quickens. The Count goes to check Susanna's story that Cherubino is not in the dressing room. Susanna reassures the Countess, who makes the most of the situation. The Count is appropriately contrite, and the section ends with all three in accord. The main thematic material consists of two contrasting themes heard in the orchestra which are fully developed during the scene.

At this crucial moment Figaro appears summoning the company to the wedding festivities in cheerful music [28] in a bright G major. But the Count sees the opportunity to get further confirmation of Susanna's story, and begins questioning his servant. Matching the insistent probing of the questioner and the hesitation of Figaro, the music changes key and slows down [30]. With the prompting of the women Figaro fends off, but does not convince the Count, who looks for the arrival of Marcellina to enforce her legal rights on Figaro to marry her.

But the next arrival is Antonio, the gardener, with his tale of a man jumping from the window onto his flower pots. This time it is Figaro's turn to improvise a story for the increasingly suspicious Count. Throughout the episode the orchestra keeps up a bubbling stream of triplets. Then the tempo assumes a more deliberate pace, as Antonio's tale becomes more circumstantial and Figaro's ingenuity is stretched to the limit. Figaro finally succeeds in giving satisfactory answers to all the Count's questions and his relief is matched by a triumphant resolution in the music [31]. But the final scene, in which Marcellina, Bartolo and Basilio erupt onto the stage, brings yet another change of fortune. Marcellina's legal rights are apparently inescapable, and all the manoeuvrings of Figaro and his allies are in vain. The Act is brought to a vivid musical climax involving all the principal characters in a septet.

Act Three opens with the continued weaving of the plot in recitative. In the duetto which follows, the Count presses the apparently complaisant Susanna, who is nervously distracted. To the Count's repeated questions she twice gives the wrong answer, and has to correct herself. The Count's insistence is well conveyed in the opening minor key, with its chromatic inflections [32], and his relief in the transition to the major [33]. Like so much else in the opera, the touching unanimity of the two characters in the closing bars has its ironical implications.

But the Count overhears a remark from Susanna to Figaro, and realizes he is being duped. The accompaniment to his recitative lends weight and an ominous significance to his soliloquy. Although as a count he has officially renounced his *droit de seigneur,* his arrogance as a man rebels at the idea that his servant may enjoy what he cannot, and the following aria expresses his feelings in violent terms. Mozart uses the stock-in-trade effects for such a situation: rushing unison scales, leaps, trills, dynamic contrasts, and a testing, wide-ranging vocal line [34, 35]. The aria reminds us of the underlying current of intolerance and violence, barely held in check, in the opera.[3]

The sestetto that follows is another instance of entrancing situation comedy. Disguises, misunderstandings, unexpected revelations of identity are the very stuff of eighteenth-century opera. No example is more appropriately placed or wittily handled than this discovery that not only is Figaro the son of Marcellina; his

3 Mozart wrote a higher version of the final section of this aria, to the same words, for Francesco Albertarelli, the Count at the 1789 Vienna revival [Ed.].

father is none other than Bartolo. The scene begins with music of graceful tenderness [36], as Marcellina embraces her long-lost son, and Figaro responds. Strings and woodwind enhance the reunion with their counterpoints. Susanna's entry and incredulity leads to more agitated music [37]. But the peace of the opening returns as Marcellina explains the truth to her. Dramatically right, this return shows Mozart's consummate ability to vary the detail of his initial material on its return. The final passage shows Mozart's profound understanding of vocal ensemble and repays detailed consideration. According to Michael Kelly, who sang Don Curzio, the 'stuttering judge', in the first performance, this was Mozart's own favourite piece in the opera.

The next scene belongs to the Countess. Apprehensive about her role in the plot to expose the Count, she recalls the days of their early untroubled love. Just as the Count's position and character were underlined by accompanied recitative, so here instrumental support is applied to extend the musings of the devoted but neglected Countess. And her second aria 'Dove sono i bei momenti' ('Where are those happy moments') [38] beautifully embodies the nobility and tenderness of her character. The simple melodic outline of the opening is embellished with gently leaning appoggiaturas, and supported by delicate touches of strings and wind. The mention of 'tears and grief' includes darker harmonies. But the opening mood returns and leads into a quick section in which she expresses her determination to win back her husband's affections.[4]

Susanna rejoins the Countess, and they compose the note of assignation for the Count, Susanna writing to the Countess's dictation. Despite their difference in social rank, the two women are sisters under the skin, and this duet is utterly charming in its atmosphere of conspiratorial intimacy [39]. Against the quietly rocking string accompaniment the woodwind share the supple flowing melodic line with the two singers. Once again a duet gives us additional insight into two of the characters.

4 Mozart also revised this aria for the 1789 revival in Vienna, when the Countess was sung by Caterina Cavalieri. The slow opening section was reduced in length, and the Allegro enlarged and provided with more brilliant coloratura [Ed.].

The mood of light-heartedness continues with the following chorus. The ingenuous singing of the village maidens is adorned by the orchestra, and the Countess gently mocks the disguised Cherubino. The advent of the Count changes the atmosphere again. His suspicions are again aroused; but Figaro, confident that the marriage will now take place, brushes them aside, and leads them into the wedding festivities that form the Finale of the Act.

Musically the Finale comprises three elements. The march [41] begins as a background to the continuing conversation. It is composed of the simplest thematic ideas, yet has its distinctive flavour distilled out of the harmony and the orchestration. Its effect is enhanced by the rise in dynamic level from a distant *pp* to a triumphant climax. The ensuing duet is carried along by its bustling accompaniment, and it too ends with a brilliant C major flourish.

In both of these pieces Mozart's imaginative economy of instrumentation is evident. But in this respect the dance movement that follows surpasses them both [43]. The fandango is in origin a Spanish courtship dance. Like other dances of popular origin it rose in the world and became fashionable among the aristocracy in the late eighteenth century. Gluck used a popular example in the ballet *Don Juan* of 1761. Mozart took the same melody in a different guise and incorporated it into this Finale. It is an extraordinarily haunting piece, stylized yet expressive, poised yet flowing. And never has a semitone been used more effectively that in the two-note counterpoint reiterated by flute, oboe and bassoon. Against this background Susanna gives the Count the letter she and the Countess have composed. As he opens it, he pricks his finger with the pin – a suggestive incident observed by Figaro. Then all join in the festivities, to the music of the duet and chorus.

The beginning of Act Four is in total contrast. Barbarina is searching for the lost pin, in a state of growing apprehension. The discrepancy between the apparently trivial loss and the emotion it induces has a comic dimension. But Barbarina's anxiety, conveyed precisely by the muted strings, the gently throbbing accompaniment and the breathless, poignantly shaped phrases of the melodic line, is all too real [44].

The next aria is allocated to Marcellina. It is often omitted, which is doubly regrettable, as it is both interesting in itself and also allows Marcellina to be seen as a more positive figure. The choice of *tempo di minuetto* underlines her courtly aspirations, the sudden bursts of coloratura her slightly comic pretentiousness [45, 46]. And if she complains rather repetitiously about the perfidy of men, she may have her reasons. Basilio's aria, too, is not often heard. He retells an amusing fable to explain his adoption of the pose of a fool [47, 48]. The loss of this rather lengthy number is less to be regretted than that of its companion piece. Perhaps the smooth hypocrisy of the character is too innate, too subtle to be explained away in this manner.[5]

Meanwhile the intrigue has developed. Figaro now suspects his wife of intended infidelity. He calls on Bartolo and Basilio to be discreet witnesses of her misconduct and expresses his bitterness in a recitative and aria. This is his moment of strongest feeling, when he sees his situation, understandably from his point of view, as tragic. The string accompaniment in the recitative underlines his alternating grief and outrage.

In the aria he inveighs bitterly against the faithlessness of women, in strongly accented music of wide-ranging compass and angular leaps [49]. In the closing bars the horns add to his torment with their mocking comments. His state of mind is not improved when Susanna, realizing he is within earshot, decides to confirm his suspicions. In her recitative and aria she expresses her impatience at her lover's delay, in music which combines simplicity and longing [50], with an accompaniment deftly scored for woodwind and pizzicato strings.[6]

In the Finale all the complexities of the plot are unravelled. Cherubino declares his love to the Countess, thinking her to be Susanna [52]. He is discovered by the Count, and makes off. It is now the Count's turn to make advances to the supposed Susanna.

5 Both of these arias are now heard with increasing frequency in performance as greater fidelity to the original intentions of the composer have become more valued [Ed.].

6 Mozart replaced the aria 'Deh vieni, non tardar' with the extended rondò with obbligato wind 'Al desio di chi t'adora' ('To the desire of one who adores you') K577 for Adriana Ferraresi in the 1789 Vienna revival. See Libretto, p. 294 and Thematic Guide music example [51], p. 81 [Ed.].

But he too is interrupted, by Figaro. Figaro notices another woman, and is not deceived by Susanna's disguise. He turns the tables on her, by pretending to make love to her as the Countess. She attempts to maintain her impersonation, but her rising indignation gets the better of her, and she boxes the delighted Figaro's ear. He confesses that he recognized her, and together they determine to maintain the charade for the Count's benefit. The sight of his servant apparently making advances to his wife enrages him and he swears vengeance. But the real Countess abandons her disguise. The Count is shamed into begging his wife for forgiveness [57]. This she grants, not for the first and probably not for the last time. The opera ends with general celebrations.

Each of Mozart's great operas has its unique personality; each helps us to understand some aspects of the human condition. *Don Giovanni* treats of love, lust and the destructive power of pride. *Così fan tutte* examines the connection between social mask and personal feeling. *Die Zauberflöte* explores the meaning of symbolism, the problem of putting idealism into practice. *Le nozze di Figaro* contains something of all of these; and more besides. It is a study of a wide range of individuals interacting in a recognizable social situation. That the range is so comprehensive, crossing social boundaries without obscuring them, is in the first instance due to the comprehensive perception of Beaumarchais, who created a sharply delineated group of personalities in complex, interlocking and developing relationships. The operatic collaborators, with an infallible certainty of touch, used their medium to humanize still further the writer's creations. The reduction of the intellectual dimension of the play is more than compensated for by the extraordinarily real emotional interplay in the opera. It is the combination of variety, vividness and naturalness of characterization that makes *Figaro*, for many, the most memorable, the most exhilarating and the greatest of all social comedies.

Recitatives in *Figaro*: Some Thoughts

David Syrus

The action in Mozart's operas is often advanced by secco recitatives for voice and continuo. How these should be delivered is a subject of some conjecture. Here are some thoughts from a conductor and seasoned répétiteur with long experience of working on all the major Mozart operas.

There is much evidence that eighteenth-century secco recitatives should be inflected with speech rhythms, rather than the rhythm of the composed notes. In 1762 Carl Philipp Emanuel Bach wrote 'the rhythm is written because of orthography; you must not observe it'.[1] In 1780 Johann Adam Hiller wrote 'everyone knows that always and everywhere recitative is sung without observation of the bar'.[2] Luigi Bassi, Mozart's first Don Giovanni, said everything 'should be parlando and almost improvised; Mozart wanted it so.'[3] And there are many other similar contemporary commentaries.

Even without this authorization, we could guess that the notation was not meant to be binding. The recitatives use a much narrower musical vocabulary than the arias, duets, trios and ensembles. They are always in common time ($\frac{4}{4}$, i.e. four crotchets in a bar), there is no tempo mark, and they use only three lengths of note (crotchets, quavers and semiquavers). Note values available to them but not used include: dotted notes, which lengthen the main note by half again (there are a very few of these in the other Da Ponte operas but none in *Figaro*); ties, which can make up new lengths by joining notes together; and compound metre, where the basic pulse is divided into threes rather than twos or fours.

1 C.P.E. Bach, *Versuch über die wahre Art das Klavier zu spielen* (Berlin, 1762).

2 Johann Adam Hiller, *Anweisung zum musikalisch-zierlichen Gesange* (Leipzig, 1780).

3 Daniel Heartz, *Mozart's Operas* (Berkeley: University of California Press, 1990) p. 172.

Once we have freed ourselves from the printed rhythm, we can of course insert extra pauses (rests) where the text punctuation implies it, and by the same logic not feel obliged to observe rests in the given material (they may well only be there to fill up the $\frac{4}{4}$ bar). This latter freedom is, in my experience, the one that literal-minded singers find hardest to take on board. I suggest that this may be the result of exposure to too many pedantic répétiteurs at a formative age…

So are these recitatives totally open to our imagination and experiments? Well, I feel not, though many present-day singers and directors consider they have total licence. The recitatives are declaimed over a harmonic structure which tells us quite a lot about the direction and emphasis of the texts, and I should like to point out some of these factors.

The accompaniment is on a chord-playing instrument, mostly harpsichord, but also at times fortepiano, strengthened on the bass line, depending on taste, by a cello. The cello can also play chords to convey harmony. Mozart positions these interventions very carefully, and they introduce both rhythmic and harmonic factors. Tonal harmony, in this period, is based on triads, the superimposing of two notes, one a third higher, one a fifth, above each note in the scale. Above a C, therefore, we would have an E and G, and this basic format is called root position ($\binom{5}{3}$). If we play the same three notes with the E at the bottom, we have the first inversion ($\binom{6}{3}$). In theory we could have, on G, a second inversion, but this never appears in recitatives. When we have a chord on the dominant, the second most important pitch in any key, we may at times add a fourth note (a seventh above the main note). If these notes are arranged with the seventh at the bottom, this is a third inversion ($\begin{pmatrix}6\\4\\2\end{pmatrix}$). Of the various positions of the chords, root position ($\binom{5}{3}$) does not need to go anywhere – it can be final, and indeed almost every recitative ends with a cadence of two root position chords affirming the key of the new number. Not counting these final cadences, there are around 450 chords in the *Figaro* recitatives, and of these some 260 are $\frac{6}{3}$ chords, well over half. These are chords which imply that more is to come. Around 150 are $\frac{5}{3}$ chords, the ones that can signify a full stop and the end of something.

How does this work out dramatically? One illustration could be given in Act One when the Count quizzes Cherubino on how he came to be in the chair. 'Ma s'io stesso m'assisi / quando in camera entrai!' ('But I sat down there myself when I came into the room!') he probes, over $^{6}_{3}$ chords, and Cherubino hopes to put an end to the questioning, over $^{5}_{3}$ chords, with 'Ed allora di dietro io mi celai ('Then I hid myself behind it'). This happens three times, indicated by the circled numbers 1, 2 and 3 in the following:

Similarly, at the start of the opera, Susanna, with two $^{6}_{3}$s, asks Figaro 'Cosa stai misurando / caro il mio Figaretto?' ('What are you measuring, / my dearest Figaro?'). He replies with a $^{5}_{3}$ 'Io guardo se quel letto / che ci destina il Conte / farà buona figura in questo loco' ('I'm seeing if this bed / which the Count has put aside for us / will go well just here'), the chord implying that the answer is complete and nothing more need be said. Susanna says 'E in questa stanza?' ('In this room?') and the following discussion, all on $^{6}_{3}$s, wanders fast through an assortment of keys, before Figaro reinstates a $^{5}_{3}$ (in the same key as when he started!) saying 'Guarda un poco / se potriasi star meglio in altro loco' ('just see / if it could go better anywhere else'). He just wants an end to this conversation. I would not claim that there is only one way to play these lines, but Mozart has chosen his chords, their timing and their tonality with care, and we need to be aware of this when making decisions about how to perform these passages.

Another question arises in bar eleven of this first recitative of Act One when Susanna becomes defiant. 'E la ragione?' ('What's the matter?') asks Figaro, which Susanna declines to answer, adding 'Perché non voglio. / Sei tu mio servo o no?' ('Because I don't choose to. / Are you my servant, or not?). Mozart writes here a crisp rhythmic cadence (indicated by an x in the following example) which is harmonically superfluous, the short note merely reiterating the harmony in a different position, $^{4}_{3}$ instead of $^{6}_{3}$:

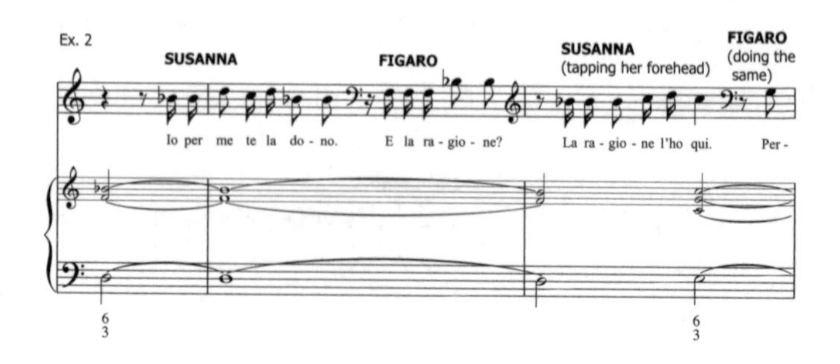

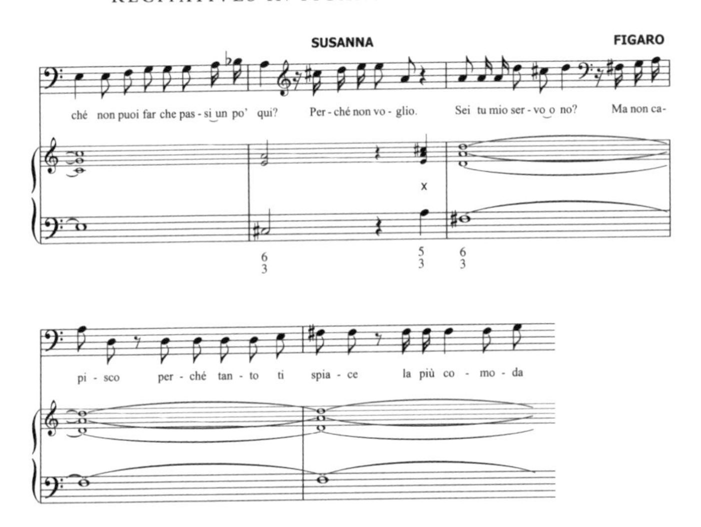

The line could in theory be played in many ways (even coquettishly perhaps?), but this repetition of the chord gives an extra shot of energy, and I think the singer must reflect that energy. There are only seven occasions in the whole of *Figaro* where Mozart repeats a chord in a different position but the same harmony. There has been a tendency (and in my early years of continuo playing I was all too guilty of it) to put such extra chords into the continuo precisely to give this extra energy, especially at cadence points. However, as Mozart has this vocabulary at his disposal and uses it very discreetly, I believe we are wrong to add the effect as an extra ourselves.

It may be well to point out that along with those seven examples there are some thirty-five uses of the $\substack{6\\4\\2}$ chord in *Figaro*, which generally serves as a repetition of a dominant (three-part) chord with the extra dimension of the added seventh. These derive in all but four instances from a linear progression in the bass line. In the following example from Act Two, the Countess asks Susanna about Cherubino, saying 'Dov'è la canzonetta?' ('Where's his song?') and Susanna responds 'Eccola: appunto / facciam che ce la canti. / Zitto, vien gente! È desso: avanti, avanti, signor uffiziale' ('Here it is: and when he comes / let's make him sing it. / Hush, someone's coming: it's he. / Come in, come in / my gallant captain'). Cherubino then arrives and says 'Ah, non chiamarmi / con nome sì fatale!' (Oh don't call me by that / horrid title!'). Here the linear use of a passing $\begin{smallmatrix}6\\4\\2\end{smallmatrix}$ happens twice, as shown here in the sequence a, b, c:

As we can see, this bass line is part of a normal scale, with the usual mixture of whole-tone steps and semitone steps from a $\begin{smallmatrix}5\\3\end{smallmatrix}$. However, in the four exceptions the bass line moves chromatically from a $\begin{smallmatrix}6\\3\end{smallmatrix}$, which has a more insinuating (even slimy) effect. The first three are all associated with Cherubino (he sings over the first, and is sung about by Basilio and the Countess in the other two). The fourth statement is part of the lascivious conversation between the

Count and Susanna at the start of Act Three, ending with Susanna's flirtatious 'È mio dovere' ('It's my duty'). The chromatic shift is shown by x:

Now, we don't necessarily need the bass line to tell us that this is an erotic conversation; but we might be tempted to deliver the Count's line aggressively or resentfully if we only knew the text. I would suggest that the sliding bass line requires us to sing the line suggestively.

How much the linear, horizontal aspect of the bass line can or should be shown depends a lot on whether a cello is used. If it is, then the pairs of notes, as in example 1 above, can be pointed up: play the open-ended note (with the $^{6}_{3}$) long, and play the decisive close (the $^{5}_{3}$) short, for example. When Mozart writes a succession of $^{6}_{3}$s, the pacing is pretty much up for grabs, as long as we don't imply that it is the end of something. To imply that sort of finality is a solecism along the lines of directors who give Fiordiligi or the Queen of the Night a false exit halfway through their arias; these pieces could not end there, they are in the wrong key, so the move looks false and stagey. Of course, we can occasionally play against expectations (though we shouldn't overdo the effect); when in Act Two the Count invites the Countess to leave with him, 'Andiamo' ('Let's go'), it is on a $^{6}_{3}$, open-ended, waiting for her to finish with a $^{5}_{3}$:

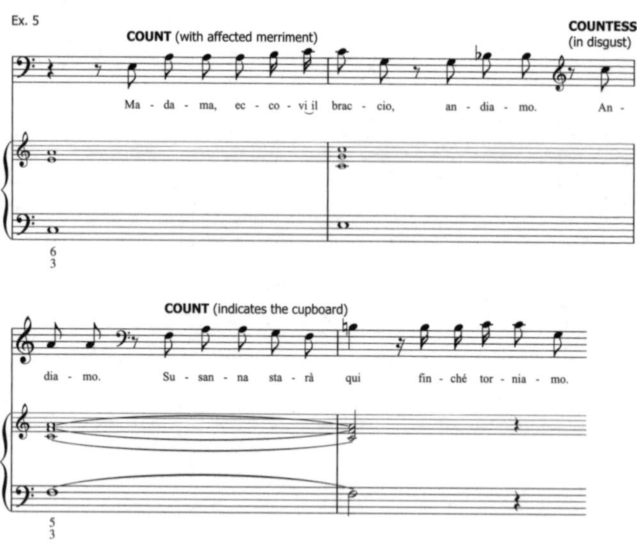

This is not an order from him, although Mozart could indeed have composed his line onto a $^{5}_{3}$, implying that there is no option open. As it is, the Countess can certainly keep the Count waiting for her answer if she wishes, and there will be dramatic tension in wondering when (or whether) she will eventually reply. But the music tells us that she will say something, that she will not sweep out of the room without a word. And this she duly does, repeating 'Andiamo'. Here and throughout the piece Mozart the dramatist is engaged in every bar, and our freedoms in the inflection of the recitative must always be bounded by these harmonic and rhythmic clues he is giving us. If there are any regrets in my four decades of happy experiment with these great operas of Mozart, it is that all too few directors – indeed, sadly, all too few conductors – listen to these expressive and informative bass lines. Whatever our position on how many notes the keyboard player should actually play, these timings and these harmonies must be made clear.

Music and Comedy in *Le nozze di Figaro*

Stephen Oliver

Explaining the point of other people's jokes is a dreary business: but do not be alarmed, I do not mean to do quite that. After all, Mozart's individual strokes of humour are models of clarity. We all rejoice in the Count's discovery of Cherubino hiding in the armchair; and it is not until we have stopped laughing that we realize with what meticulous care the moment has been exposed for us. No sudden shock; no whisking off the covers; no great bangs on the orchestra: but slow, soft, creeping music, as the people on the stage gradually realize the significant ironies of the situation. This realization needs time; and Mozart gives it plenty of time. He even allows us to laugh without having to drown a single word, by putting a silent pause after Basilio's incomparable:

And this sense of clarity pays dividends when Mozart is dealing with purely verbal jokes. In a comedy about marriage and sex, it's not surprising that now and then his characters make suggestive remarks, like the Count's

or Figaro's

del - le bel - le tur - ban - do il ri - po - so,

To make sure everyone picks up the words at these points, nothing in the least elaborate is permitted to get in the way of the text. The orchestra merely plays along with the voice part in octaves. But these plain octaves themselves take on significance. They somehow sound salacious; it's perhaps something to do with the very careful off-beat phrasing of:

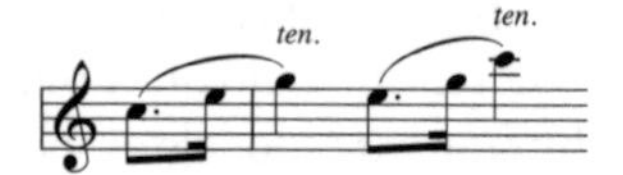
ten.
ten.

Here, what doubtless began as a technical device – a method of getting the words over clearly – ends as a dramatic reinforcement. The octaves admirably express the over-significant tone – 'Nudge, nudge, wink, wink' – that people adopt at such moments.

We recognize the tone of voice here – we have all made such jokes in just such a way. And this recognition makes the music real to us as well as funny. It is like that moment when Susanna harps on Marcellina's age:

L'e - tà! l'e - tà! l'e - tà!

We recognize the rhetoric of the playground:

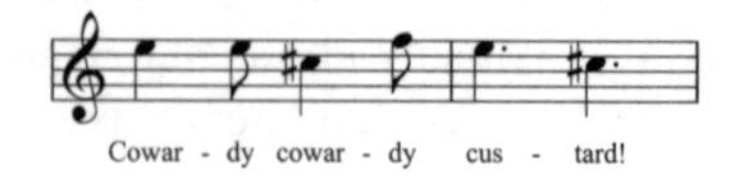
Cowar - dy cowar - dy cus - tard!

and are amused, and perhaps a little ashamed of ourselves as well. This makes for great comedy, this touching as well as amusing us — and we can all pick out moments in *Figaro* where we are touched and delighted at the same time like that. My own favourite, for what it's worth, is the self-disgust and embarrassment of Figaro's interruption of his own cadence in his Act Four aria:

That stabbing high D flat (x marks the spot in my example) as another wave of shame and anger breaks over him is horribly real.

But these are all individual moments; and merely stringing such insights together will not make an opera. So what is it that makes *Figaro* – the whole opera – so satisfactory, so amusing, so invigorating a work?

We think at first of tunes. How could an opera with such tunes as 'Dove sono i bei momenti' ('Where are those happy moments') [38], 'Voi che sapete / che cosa è amor' ('You ladies / who know what love is') [19] and 'Deh vieni, non tardar' ('Come, do not delay') [50] in it be anything other than a masterpiece? Well, it may be heresy to say so, but I don't think Mozart's melodies, simply as melodies, to be uniquely beautiful. They are distinguished, of course; incomparably orchestrated and finished: but the achievement of the tunes themselves can be equalled in many another eighteenth-century opera.

If it is not the tunes or the individual jokes alone that make the music of this opera so satisfying, what is it then? We open the score: the conductor raises his baton: and the pianissimo quavers begin [1]. Consider for a moment that phrase which opens the Overture. Apart from anything else, merely as the start of an overture it's unusual enough. Most comic operas before or since have begun their overtures with a loud bang, not with this soft surreptitious scurrying of mere surprise. It is rapid, secretive; the music of intrigues and whispers. There is a suggestion of harmonic tension too – when the phrase is repeated twenty seconds later, the woodwind provide a discord on every main beat. And this tension immediately explodes in a loud answering phrase, itself sufficiently discordant:

The way the music proceeds, in fact, is by building up tensions and immediately releasing them, those releases themselves becoming a source for new tensions. The music is, literally, progressive – not in the sense that it is modern for its time; but in that it is built so that it never relaxes, because each phrase is always pressing forward into the next.

But doesn't all music work like that? Am I merely imagining this particular source of tension? Look at another Mozart overture, superficially built on the same lines – that to *Così fan tutte*. It begins quite differently; here, indeed, we have the conventional loud opening in the easiest of harmonic styles, merely alternating between tonic and dominant. But even when it starts sounding a bit like *Figaro* – in the following fast section – the likeness is only superficial. The actual musical phrases, to be sure, are not at all unlike those of *Figaro* – a soft rapid movement round a note followed by loud passages with trumpets and drums. But the tension of the *Figaro* harmony is not in the *Così* overture at all – in *Così*, the strings frankly settle down to an easy um-cha-cha-cha rhythm, and the woodwind merely chuckle above them.

Or for an even clearer example of the way tension is built into the music of *Figaro*, compare its opening scene with that of *Così*. *Così* actually begins with a quarrel; and here, at any rate, you might expect the music to be tense and energetic. Not at all: the opening tune blandly outlines the common chord:

Turn in contrast to *Figaro*. The curtain goes up. A domestic scene: a man measuring a room, a girl trying on a hat. Nothing like a quarrel or even an argument. But listen to the music. Every phrase has a discord built into it – this sort of thing:

and later this:

And by such means a sense of tension is continually kept up throughout the whole duet.

You will have seen for some time what I'm driving at. I believe *Figaro* to be so satisfying an experience not just because of the tunes or the jokes, agreeable as they are. Rather it is because the texture of the music is so highly wrought – works at so high a level of tension – that the energy thus generated presses us through the opera's considerable length with an unremitting sense of expectation and delight. The opera remains exciting because of the tensions generated by the music.

Why, after all, did the audience at the first dress rehearsal of Act One, in 1786, go so wild at the end of 'Non più andrai, farfallone amoroso' ('No more, you amorous butterfly') [16], its final number? Of course, it's something of an applause-catcher in itself, with its trumpets and drums and shouts of 'Cherubino alla vittoria!' ('Cherubino, on to victory'). But in its context it carries a more formidable effect.

Every number in the first act has been pitched at a high level of excitement. To start with, over half of them are dramatic ensembles of one sort or another, in which the action sweeps forward. But even the solo songs are highly energized. The elegant measured rhythm of the minuet becomes explosive in Figaro's 'Se vuol ballare, signor Contino' ('If, my dear Count, / You feel like dancing') [7]. Horns and plucked strings combine to paint a remarkable picture of suppressed resentment. The off-beat clarinets and chromatically rising strings of 'Non so più cosa son, cosa faccio' ('I no longer know what I am or what I'm doing') [12] vividly convey Cherubino's constant state of sensual arousal. And the trumpets and drums of Bartolo's old-fashioned peroration build up the tension of the moment when joined with the furious pace of his patter. Even the little chorus, quaintly pastoral though it is, becomes a dangerous weapon in the struggle between Figaro and his master.

At the end of all this screwing up of tension comes 'Non più andrai'. Here, the tune is simplicity itself, merely outlining the chords on which it's based. The phrase lengths are evenly balanced, and mostly grouped in pairs. There is no chromaticism; and the modulations are of the most obvious kind. The rondo form is simple and clear. Everything in the song is straightforward and direct. And thus, with a rush, the tension of the whole Act is released. The simple idea of a vigorous, martial tune, combined with its placing at the end of a complicated Act, makes its effect doubly strong. Music and drama fuse together in a moment of theatrical power possible only to opera.

No wonder the audience at that dress rehearsal, obscurely recognizing this, leapt up with cries of congratulation; and the little man, smiling ecstatically, bowed again and again from his seat at the harpsichord. To have brought off so complicated and subtle an effect and to do it with such apparent simplicity and ease is a mark of the highest skill. Doubtless Mozart, if not his audience, knew that perfectly well.

And I must not forget that this skill is here addressing itself to the purposes of comedy. For *Figaro* is extremely funny; and funny because of the intensity and energy of the music. Whether it is the accompanying triplets of 'Via resti servita' ('After you') [11] surging to the top of the texture as the two women exchange insults; or the deliberate, constant, almost menacing tread of the fandango bass as letters are passed and fingers are pricked; or the horns – cuckold's horns – jeering at poor Figaro as he inveighs against all women – it is always the power of the music that makes the comedy. It has often been pointed out, for instance, how the romantic beauty of Susanna's 'Deh vieni' creates, by its being overheard by Figaro, a highly charged irony. For although Figaro thinks otherwise, it is really he whom Susanna is serenading, after all.

This brings us, indeed, to the other main way by which the music provides for the comedy. *Figaro* is at some moments a farcical play, rapidly moving from situation to situation; so energy and tension in the music is very much to be desired. But it is also a play about love, about feeling; and this, not in the mere writing of tunes, is really where the richness and elegance of Mozart's language finds its purpose. The Countess's Act Two aria 'Porgi, amor, qualche ristoro'' ('O love, bring some relief') [18] begins, oddly, with the same phrase as the bustling Susanna–Figaro duet 'Se a caso, madama' ('Supposing my lady') [6] of the first Act. But the discord which gave the earlier tune impetus:

now becomes a faintly self-indulgent sigh, wonderfully extended in its answering phrase:

The energy generated by the discord is still there, but transmuted to romantic sentiment.

By the Letter Duet in Act Three [39], though, all harmonic tension has disappeared. The music is as sweet as Mozart can make it; and the comedy lies wholly in the irony of the situation. The two women seek to trick the husband of one of them into decent behaviour by tempting him to adultery with the other, 'Ei già il resto capirà' ('The rest he'll understand'), they say; and the setting of the remark by Mozart changes its bitterness into an inevitable and accepted sorrow.

The music, in other places informing the situation with energy, here provides a moment of reflective beauty. It is in these two ways that the comedy as comedy finally lives. The jokes, the tunes, the natural turns of speech are all subsumed in music of equal energy and loveliness.

And this is surely an odd thing. Everyone knows that Beaumarchais's *Figaro* was a conventional type of plot brought to new life, partly by injecting a little romantic sensibility into it, to be sure, but mostly by injecting a great deal of savage social satire. This whole comic method – the oldest indeed of comic methods, extending certainly back to Aristophanes – Mozart calmly ignores. There is practically no social satire in the opera. Mozart was far too absorbed in the contemplation of his people, his Count and Countess, his gardeners and chambermaids and pages, to satirize them. No doubt he had his own views on their behaviour, but they cannot be said to intrude upon the opera. Merely presenting his people as vividly as he can will be interesting and amusing enough.

Here falls into place one of Mozart's purely arbitrary pieces of luck. He was working at a time when people still enjoyed the old comedies of situation, requiring them merely to be infused with good feeling to be made new. Nothing could have been more fortunate for an opera composer. He had no need to waste time setting up conventions; the conventions were well understood: and he could confine himself to filling them with what new life his genius prompted him to. Too much life for his contemporaries, perhaps – 'Too many notes, my dear Mozart' said Emperor Leopold of the 1782 Singspiel *Die Entführung aus dem Serail* – but for us the energy and temper of the music make of the comedy's rather faded colours an invigorating and enduring delight.

A Selective Performance History

George Hall

Le nozze di Figaro had its premiere on 1st May 1786 at the Burgtheater in Vienna; Mozart himself led the performance from the keyboard. The cast consisted of regular members of the *opera buffa* company established at the venue in 1783: Luisa Laschi (Countess), Nancy Storace (Susanna), Dorotea Bussani (Cherubino), Maria Mandini (Marcellina), Anna Gottlieb (Barbarina), Stefano Mandini (Count), Francesco Benucci (Figaro), Francesco Bussani (Bartolo/Antonio) and Michael Kelly (Basilio/Don Curzio).

Born in Florence some time in the 1760s, the soprano Luisa Laschi (playing the Countess and perhaps in her late twenties) had first sung in Vienna in 1783, and appeared as Rosina in Giovanni Paisiello's setting of *Il barbiere di Siviglia* – an obvious progenitor to Mozart's opera – in 1785. Her marriage to the tenor Domenico Mombelli drew the following *Figaro*-inspired jocularity from Emperor Joseph II writing to his chamberlain, Count Rosenberg, on 29th September 1786: 'The marriage between Laschi and Mombelli may take place without waiting for my return, and I cede to you *le droit de seigneur.*' Her later Viennese creations included Martín y Soler's *Una cosa rara* (1786) and *L'arbore di Diana* (1787) as well as Antonio Salieri's *Axur, re d'Ormus* (1788). In May of that year she sang Zerlina in the first Viennese performance of *Don Giovanni*. She seems to have made her farewell appearance in the city in 1789 and died about 1790, though exactly when and where is not known.

Ann (also Anna or Nancy) Storace (Susanna, aged twenty-one) was an English soprano and the sister of the composer Stephen Storace.

Born in London in 1765, she was singing professionally by the age of seven. She studied with such luminaries as the castrato Venanzio Rauzzini and the composer Antonio Sacchini before – following her brother's example – heading for Italy. Her continental career began in Florence in 1779 and she was soon singing in the major Italian centres, creating a role in Giuseppe Sarti's *Fra i due litiganti il terzo gode* in Milan in 1782. Her success in Venice led to her being hired for the newly formed Viennese *opera buffa* company the following year. A popular and well-paid artist, she premiered many new works by locally based composers, including Martín y Soler (*Una cosa rara*) as well as Mozart and her brother; in addition Mozart wrote for her the concert aria *Ch'io mi scordi di te?*, in which he played the piano obbligato at her Viennese farewell concert in 1787. She then returned to London to become a mainstay of operatic life in the English capital, including in a sequence of works written by her brother; she also sang regularly in oratorios and concerts in London and other musical centres. She retired in 1808 and died in Dulwich in 1817. As a specialist in comic roles, she was described by the knowledgeable amateur Lord Mount Edgcumbe as 'in her particular line [...] unrivalled, being an excellent actress as well as a masterly singer'.

Dorotea Bussani (Cherubino, aged twenty-two or twenty-three) was the only native Viennese in the cast. Born in 1763, she married Francesco Bussani some five weeks before the *Figaro* premiere. A member of the Burgtheater company throughout its history, she also created the role of Fidalma in Dominico Cimarosa's *Il matrimonio segreto* (1792). Feeling themselves undervalued, the Bussanis left Vienna in 1794 and made their way to Italy, but they were back by 1796. Dorotea sang in Lisbon in 1807–09, and later in London. She died some time after 1810.

Little is known of the soprano Maria Mandini (Marcellina) other than that she was French and the daughter of an official at Versailles. The wife of the baritone Stefano Mandini, she joined the Viennese company at the same time as her husband and created operas by Martín y Soler as well as Mozart's *Figaro*. Nothing is recorded of her life beyond the performing dates 1782–91; after the break-up of the Viennese company husband and wife sang in Naples and Paris.

Anna Gottlieb (Barbarina) was only twelve years old when she created the role of Barbarina, though as the child of a Viennese theatrical family she had first appeared at the Burgtheater seven years earlier. Later she moved to Emanuel Schikaneder's company at the Freihaus-Theater (replaced by the nearby Theater an der Wien in 1799), where she created Pamina in *Die Zauberflöte* in 1791. From 1792 onwards she centred her career on Singspiel at the suburban Theater in der Leopoldstadt, where her contract was finally terminated in 1828; she lived on until the Mozart centenary year of 1856, dying in Vienna at the age of eighty-two.

Maria Mandini's husband Stefano, the first Count (aged thirty-five or thirty-six), is better documented than his wife. Born in 1750, he was singing in Ferrara in 1774 and was hired, together with Maria, as one of the founding members of the Viennese enterprise. Among his previous roles with the company were Count Almaviva in Paisiello's *Il barbiere di Siviglia* (originally written for tenor) and the creation of the title role in the same composer's *Il re Teodoro in Venezia* (1784); further creations included the Poet in Salieri's *Prima la musica e poi le parole* (1786) as well as *Una cosa rara*, *L'arbore di Diana* and *Axur, re d'Ormus*. He is believed to have died around 1810.

A leading light of the company, the bass-baritone Francesco Benucci (Figaro, roughly aged forty) was born around 1745 and active from at least 1769. In Vienna his creations were many: Storace's *Gli sposi malcontenti* (1785), *Una cosa rara*, and Salieri's *La scuola de' gelosi* (1783), *La grotta di Trofonio* (1785) and the title role in *Axur*; he was also the first Viennese Leporello, the first Guglielmo in *Così fan tutte* (1790) and the first Count Robinson in *Il matrimonio segreto*. He sang the Count/Susanna duet 'Crudel! Perché finora' with Nancy Storace in a performance of Giuseppe Gazzaniga's *La vendemmia* in London in 1789 – apparently the first piece from *Figaro* to be heard on the UK stage. He died in Florence in 1824. His colleague Michael Kelly remembered him rehearsing 'Non più andrai' under Mozart who, '*sotto voce*, was repeating, Bravo! Bravo! Bennuci [sic] [...] and when Bennuci came to the fine passage, "Cherubino, alla vittoria, alla gloria militar", which he gave out with stentorian lungs, the effect was electricity itself'.

His compatriot Francesco Bussani (Bartolo/Antonio, aged forty-two or forty-three) was born in Rome in 1743. He first sang as a tenor, but by 1777 was one of Italy's leading bass-baritones. In Vienna, where he worked from 1783 to 1794, he was engaged as a stage manager as well as a singer; Da Ponte's Memoirs complain of his intrigues even during the *Figaro* rehearsals. He had directed the premiere of Mozart's *Der Schauspieldirektor* earlier in 1786, and sang two roles (Masetto and the Commendatore) in the first Viennese *Don Giovanni*, as well as creating Don Alfonso in *Così*. By 1795 he was back in Italy, where his career continued for some years; he is last heard of in 1807 in Lisbon, where his wife was performing.

Michael Kelly (Basilio/Don Curzio, aged twenty-three) was one of the most colourful as well as best recorded (mostly by himself) of the premiere cast. Born in Dublin in 1762, he was singing there professionally in 1777, two years before his departure for Naples for further study. He made his debut in 1781 in Florence and like Storace was recruited by the Austrian ambassador to Venice for the new Viennese project. He was a second (or comic) tenor, though clearly useful to the company, creating roles in *Gli sposi malcontenti*, *Una cosa rara* and Storace's *Gli equivoci* (1786) as well as *Figaro*. Returning to London with Storace in 1787, he too joined the company at Drury Lane in a succession of English operas, several of them by Stephen Storace, occasionally appearing at the King's Theatre. Lord Mount Edgcumbe was critical of aspects of his Drury Lane performances: 'Though he was a good musician and not a bad singer, having been long in Italy, yet he had retained, or regained, so much of the English vulgarity of manner that he was never greatly liked.' From 1793 he worked as a stage manager at the King's Theatre, continuing to hold this post for more than thirty years. He also contributed, as a composer, to numerous stage works, though his compatriot Thomas Moore was withering about his capabilities ('Poor Mick is rather an imposer than a composer'). Sheridan was equally dismissive of his ventures in the wine trade. He managed to keep himself afloat until 1811, when he was declared bankrupt on the day that coincided with his final operatic appearance. He died in Margate in 1826.

* * *

Le nozze di Figaro was an immediate success. Mozart's father Leopold described in a letter to his daughter Nannerl how 'at the second performance of your brother's opera five pieces and at the third performance seven pieces were encored, including a duettino ['Aprite, presto, aprite'] that was sung three times.' Corroboration comes from a ban imposed on encores following the third performance to prevent the evening going on too long. *Figaro* was given an additional outing at the Laxenburg Palace on 24th May.

Following a revival later in the year in Vienna it disappeared from the local repertory until August 1789, when Mozart made some alterations to accommodate changes in the cast. The Count's aria was revised (probably for Francesco Albertarelli), while the new Susanna, Adriana Ferrarese (1759–after 1803), required two substitute numbers: 'Un moto di gioia' replaced 'Venite inginocchiatevi' and 'Al desio di chi t'adora' replaced 'Deh vieni, non tardar'. Ferrarese was Da Ponte's mistress, and would go on to create the role of Fiordiligi in *Così* in 1790. Mozart's view of her is encapsulated in a letter: 'the little aria ['Un moto di gioia'] I have written for [her] I believe will please, if she is capable of singing it in an artless manner, which I very much doubt.'

Meanwhile, in December 1786 *Figaro* had won an even greater success in Prague, where the *Prager Oberpostamtszeitung* announced that 'No piece (so everyone is saying) has made such an impression as the Italian opera *Le nozze di Figaro*, which the [Pasquale] Bondini company of opera virtuosos has already given with the greatest success.' Caterina Bondini sang Susanna, Felice Ponziani Figaro, and Luigi Bassi the Count. The composer's own reaction to local appreciation is well known: 'Here they talk about nothing but *Figaro*', he wrote in a letter to Baron von Jacquin. 'Nothing is played, sung or whistled but *Figaro*. No opera is drawing like *Figaro*. Nothing, nothing but *Figaro*.' Its popularity would lead to the commissioning of *Don Giovanni*, premiered in Prague in 1787. Mozart himself directed performances of *Figaro* in Prague in January 1787, and again later in the year, immediately prior to the production of his new work.

The next two productions both seem to have been come about through connections between members of the Habsburg dynasty and took place in their Italian dominions. The first was in Monza, not far from Milan, in the autumn of 1787, though for some reason the third and fourth acts were newly set by another composer, Angelo Tarchi (*c.*1760–1814). In June 1788 *Figaro* was performed at the Teatro della Pergola in Florence, though divided up into two evenings.

Many performances followed throughout German-speaking countries, though local theatres often played the opera as a Singspiel – translated into German and with spoken dialogue replacing the recitatives. The first such presentation was at the Rosenthal-Theater in Prague (June 1787). A translation by Adolf von Knigge, with dialogue translated from the French by his daughter Philippine Eregine von Knigge, made initially for a touring company, was first performed in Lübeck in May 1788 and thereafter gained wide currency; a second by Christian August Vulpius, first used in October 1788 in Frankfurt, became equally popular. The opera reached Bonn and Cologne in 1789, Stuttgart and Berlin in 1790, Hamburg in 1791, Munich in 1794 and Dresden in 1795. Foreign centres heard it in various languages and in different adaptations: Amsterdam (1794), Madrid (1802), Budapest (1812), New York (1824 – initially in English) and St Petersburg (1836 – initially in German). Tchaikovsky provided recitatives for a Russian-language version translated by his brother Modest staged at the Moscow Conservatory in 1876.

The Théâtre de l'Opéra in Paris presented *Figaro* on 20th March 1793, in French and with spoken dialogue adapted from Beaumarchais's play; it lasted just five performances. It later played at the Théâtre-Italien (from 1807) and the Théâtre Lyrique (1858). From 1872 it became a staple of the Opéra-Comique, garnering 415 performances there by 1946. A major new production of *Figaro* at the Palais Garnier was mounted only in 1973, in a celebrated staging by the Italian director Giorgio Strehler and conducted by Georg Solti that was presented first at Versailles (30th March) as the opening gambit of Rolf Liebermann's regime as general director. The critic of *Opera* magazine, Pierre Breger, was enraptured: 'Strehler's aim is total theatre. This was made possible by his having at his disposal not just a cast of fine singers but of singers physically suited for their roles. They ceased to act; they lived the roles.' With its subtle, realistic sets (by Ezio Frigerio), the staging became a regular feature of the Parisian repertoire and was also seen at La Scala, Milan, where Riccardo Muti conducted it. Latterly junked by Gerard Mortier when he became general director and replaced by a staging by Christoph Marthaler in 2006, it has subsequently been recreated, largely from photographs and the memories of Strehler's former assistants, at the behest of Mortier's successor, Nicolas Joel. It reopened at the Opéra Bastille in November 2010.

* * *

Following the presentation of a one-act version at the Pantheon in Oxford Street, London, on 2nd May 1812, the first complete professional UK performance of *Figaro* was given at the King's Theatre in the Haymarket – then London's main opera house – on 18th June. The cast included Maria Dickons (Countess), Angelica Catalani (Susanna; the leading star soprano of her day), the veteran Ludwig Fischer (Count; he had been Mozart's first Osmin in *Die Entführung aus dem Serail* in 1782), and Giuseppe Naldi (Figaro). Henry Robertson wrote in *The Examiner*: 'In its quick succession of incident, [it] gives full scope to the fancy, which teemed with delightful combinations of sound, and sprung from subject to subject, with inexhaustible freshness, vigour, and originality.'

Yet cuts were regularly instituted at the King's Theatre, as manager John Ebers recalled from his own period in charge (1821–27): 'As originally performed, the opera was found much too long for the customary time of representation, it having been composed for a theatre where the opera alone forms the business of the evening. As now performed, it is therefore curtailed considerably from the limits of the original.' Though less popular than *Don Giovanni*, *Figaro* continued to be an intermittent feature of London's Italian opera seasons throughout the nineteenth century.

An English version based on Thomas Holcroft's 1784 translation of the play and with music arranged by Henry Bishop opened at

Covent Garden on 6th March 1819. 'Overture and music are selected chiefly from Mozart's operas [sic]', announced the playbill, continuing, 'The new Musick composed, & the whole arranged & adapted to the English stage, by Mr. BISHOP.' Such additions and substitutions were in line with common practice at the time. *The Times* commented that Bishop's compositions 'suffer not a little by the comparison with Mozart; but on the whole the lovers of music will find in the opera a source of great enjoyment.' It was played at Drury Lane in German by a visiting company on 12th May 1841 and at Covent Garden in a new English version by James Robinson Planché on 15th March 1842.

Following the establishment of the Royal Italian Opera at Covent Garden in 1847, *Figaro* appeared there fairly regularly up to the first decade of the twentieth century, though remaining the second most popular Mozart opera after *Don Giovanni*. Many of the leading opera singers of the day – contracted for each season – took part. Among those names still resonating today are those of Giulia Grisi, Marietta Alboni, Antonio Tamburini (who first appeared in *Figaro* in 1847); Helen Lemmens-Sherrington, Désirée Artôt, Pauline Lucca, Jean-Baptiste Faure (1866); Thérèse Tietjens, Minnie Hauk, Charles Santley (1868); Zelia Trebelli-Bettini (1870); Marie Miolan-Carvalho (1871); Emma Albani, Victor Maurel (1873); Marcella Sembrich, Édouard de Reszke, Antonio Cotogni (1884); Emma Eames, Sigrid Arnoldson (1892); Zélie de Lussan (1897); Lillian Nordica (1898); and Marcel Journet, conducted by Hans Richter (1904).

Despite Sir Thomas Beecham's considerable Mozartian credentials, *Figaro* was less frequently performed during his *de facto* artistic directorship of Covent Garden in the interwar years than perhaps might have been expected. Before the First World War, he had superintended a Mozart Festival in 1910, including a production of *Figaro*, as part of a summer season of opera in English at His Majesty's Theatre, and he continued his endeavours later in that same year by transferring the production to his autumn season at Covent Garden. (Nigel Playfair followed his lead with a memorable English-language production at Drury Lane in 1917.) Nevertheless, the opera subsequently appeared at Covent Garden in only a handful of seasons – 1914 (with Rosa

Raisa and Maggie Teyte), 1922, 1923, 1926 (with Lotte Lehmann, Delia Reinhardt, Elisabeth Schumann and Richard Mayr, conducted by Bruno Walter) and 1936 (the latter during a visit by the Dresden State Opera) – prior to the outbreak of the Second World War.

The establishment of *Figaro*'s position as a standard repertory piece at Covent Garden dates from the post-war period. On 22nd January 1949 the two-year-old resident company presented a new staging by Peter Brook, then Director of Productions, designed by Rolf Gérard and conducted by Karl Rankl; the work has remained a fixture ever since. Over the years, Brook's staging starred such celebrated singers as Elisabeth Schwarzkopf, Irmgard Seefried, Geraint Evans, John Brownlee, Eberhard Wächter, Adele Leigh, Anna Pollak and Josephine Veasey, as well as conductors including Erich Kleiber.

The Brook production, which had been sung in English, was succeeded in 1963 by one by Oscar Fritz Schuh, designed by Teo Otto and conducted by Georg Solti, opening with Mirella Freni, Teresa Berganza and Tito Gobbi. This was sung in Italian, as have been all subsequent performances at Covent Garden. In 1971 John Copley directed a production, designed by Stefanos Lazaridis and conducted by Colin Davis, which launched the career of Kiri Te Kanawa as the Countess and also had Reri Grist and Patricia Kern in the first cast. Copley's detailed and observant staging proved durable as well as likeable. It lasted until 1987 when Johannes Schaaf's production, designed by Xenia Hausner and conducted by Bernard Haitink, replaced it. This was a deliberately more hard-hitting view of the work, with Karita Mattila's Countess shown being driven to alcoholism by her husband's neglect. The cast also included Thomas Allen and Claudio Desderi. In 1998, during the Royal Opera House's closure period, Patrick Young directed a production at the Shaftesbury Theatre, designed by Roger Butlin and conducted by Steven Sloane, initially featuring Nuccia Focile, Neal Davies and Dmitri Hvorostovsky. The next production at Covent Garden was by David McVicar in 2006, designed by Tanya McCallin and conducted by Antonio Pappano, with a cast led by Erwin Schrott, Miah Persson, Dorothea Röschmann and Gerald Finley. McVicar's staging moved the period of the opera forward to 1830 – significantly a year of revolution – but otherwise remained on traditional lines whilst introducing an unusually high level of interactive detail.

* * *

While Covent Garden (like other international houses) has now turned exclusively to the original language, vernacular productions of *Figaro* for long remained frequent elsewhere in the UK. At the Old Vic – precursor of Sadler's Wells Opera and now English National Opera – *The Marriage of Figaro* was performed on 15th January 1920 in a staging by Clive Carey that used a durable translation by the scholar (and Mozart expert) Edward J. Dent that was replaced only in 1991 at the London Coliseum by Jeremy Sams's version, originally presented under the title *Figaro's Wedding*. Carey's Old Vic staging transferred to the new Sadler's Wells company during its initial season in 1931; subsequent performances of *Figaro* occurred in 1934, 1940 and 1942 (both wartime touring productions also played outside London), 1951, 1956 and 1965, the last in a new staging by John Blatchley.

A new edition unveiled at Sadler's Wells in 1965 proved to be a turning point and a harbinger. Charles Mackerras, its conductor, was a musicologist as well as a great practical musician who had sought out early manuscripts and printed editions of the score in various libraries throughout Europe, discovering decorations and cadenzas used by singers of Mozart's day or shortly afterwards. In John Blatchley's production, which was designed by Vivienne Kernot, Mackerras's cast – including Elizabeth Harwood, Donald McIntyre and Raimund Herincx – keenly took up his findings. The result was a significant triumph that was to prove a harbinger of things to come in its use of historical stylistic studies as a foundation for modern performance practice. Later on, many other musicians would follow suit in terms of Mackerras's employment of appoggiaturas in recitatives and arias. The use of period instruments – not possible with a permanent modern-instrument orchestra such as those in most opera houses (Sadler's Wells included) – would gradually become more frequent in recordings and (where available) in live performances from the 1970s onwards. Also approved by Mackerras, in 1965 Robert Moberly and Christopher Raeburn proposed a logical revision of the traditional ordering of Act Three that was widely taken up for a period, though it has subsequently been increasingly discarded and Charles Mackerras himself towards the end of his life doubted its validity.[1]

Following Sadler's Wells Opera's transfer to the London Coliseum, and its 1974 renaming as English National Opera, further new productions were staged in 1978 (Jonathan Miller directed a cast including John Tomlinson, Lillian Watson, Valerie Masterson and Sally Burgess in a production designed by Patrick Robertson and conducted by Charles Groves), 1991 (Graham Vick's staging, designed by Richard Hudson and conducted by Paul Daniel; it was especially memorable for a last-act garden scene played in the theatrical equivalent of the cinematic day-for-night technique; Joan Rodgers sang the Countess to Cathryn Pope's Susanna, who was getting married to Bryn Terfel's Figaro), 2001 (Steven Stead and designer Matthew Deely, conducted by Jane Glover; Christopher Maltman was Figaro and Orla Boylan was the Countess), and 2006 (Olivia Fuchs and designer Yannis Thavoris, conducted by Roland Böer; with Mark Stone, Lisa Milne, Marie Arnet and Jonathan Lemalu in the cast).

Outside London, a particularly significant moment in the history not only of *Figaro*, but of Mozart's operas in the UK – and beyond – was the opening of John Christie's Glyndebourne Festival on 28th May 1934 with *Le nozze di Figaro*. The first four festivals were entirely devoted to Mozart, and *Figaro* was repeated every season until 1939. The central roles of the initial production were sung by Aulikki Rautawaara (Countess), Audrey Mildmay (Susanna; and also Mrs John Christie in real life), Luise Helletsgruber (Cherubino), Roy Henderson (Count), Willi Domgraf-Fassbänder (Figaro), Norman Allin (Bartolo) and Heddle Nash (Basilio); Fritz Busch was the conductor, Carl Ebert the director and Hamish Hamilton the designer. The performance was recorded by EMI in 1934–35 – a set that retains a classic status despite cuts that include almost all of the continuo recitatives.

1 See Julian Rushton's note on p. 85 [Ed.].

Retaining its Mozartian speciality and its predilection for *Figaro* as the iconic Glyndebourne opera, the festival restaged its favourite work in 1950 (once more directed by Carl Ebert, now designed by Rolf Gérard and conducted by Ferenc Fricsay), 1951 (Ebert again, designed by Hutchinson Scott, the conducting shared by Fritz Busch and John Pritchard), 1955 (Ebert yet again, this time with Oliver Messel's designs and conducted by Vittorio Gui), 1973 (Peter Hall, designed by John Bury and conducted by John Pritchard – a highly praised production, starring Ileana Cotrubas, Frederica von Stade, Benjamin Luxon and Elizabeth Harwood on its opening night), 1989 (a restaging by Hall, now designed by John Gunter, with Simon Rattle and the period-instrument Orchestra of the Age of Enlightenment in the pit), 1994 (Stephen Medcalf, designed by John Gunter and conducted by Bernard Haitink to reopen the new opera house on the sixtieth anniversary of the festival) and 2000 (Graham Vick, designed by Richard Hudson and conducted by Andrew Davis).

* * *

Vienna, meanwhile, has remained a bastion of Mozart performance, though one susceptible to renewal as well as tradition. Throughout the nineteenth century and into the second half of the twentieth – up to Herbert von Karajan's time, in fact – the opera was performed (like everything else) in German. Gustav Mahler included *Figaro* amongst the historic series of productions on which he collaborated with the designer Alfred Roller; their new version (including a recitative composed by Mahler himself) opened on 30th March 1906. Mahler also included *Figaro* among the eight works he conducted during his three seasons at the Metropolitan Opera in New York in 1908–10.

In the immediate post-war era, the Viennese ensemble, initially performing at alternative venues until the bombed Staatsoper itself reopened in 1955, made a speciality of Mozart's operas. Less than a year after the ending of the Second World War, *Le nozze di Figaro* was staged on 1st May 1946 as one of a series of productions that toured widely and were generally regarded as benchmarks of Mozartian style. In 1947 the company took *Figaro* (amongst other works) to

Covent Garden, with singers including such luminaries as Maria Cebotari (Countess), Irmgard Seefried (Susanna), Hilde Gueden (Cherubino), Elisabeth Hoengen (Marcellina), Hans Hotter (Count), Erich Kunz (Figaro) and Herbert Alsen (Bartolo); the performances were conducted by Josef Krips.

Festival venues that have thrived on Mozart and *Figaro* in particular during the twentieth century and into the twenty-first, in addition to Glyndebourne, include Salzburg, Aix-en-Provence and Garsington. In a performance transferred from the Vienna Court Opera and paid for by the Emperor Franz Joseph II, Mahler conducted *Figaro* during a Salzburg Mozart festival in 1906, and two years after the founding of the modern Salzburg Festival in 1920, *Figaro* featured in the first season there to include operas. A particularly acclaimed production was that by Günther Rennert and designed by Rudolf Heinrich, first staged at the Kleines Festspielhaus in 1966; its characteristically glamorous initial cast (on 25th July) included several of the leading lights of the day – Claire Watson (Countess), Reri Grist (Susanna), Ingvar Wixell (Count), Walter Berry (Figaro) and Edith Mathis (Cherubino), all under the baton of a figure regarded as the master Mozartian conductor of his time: Karl Böhm. *Figaro* joined the Mozart-led repertoire at the Aix-en-Provence festival in 1952, four years after the event was established, and has rarely left it for long. And in the UK, it was the success of an Opera 80 touring production of *Figaro* at Garsington Manor in 1989 that led Leonard Ingrams to found Garsington Opera shortly afterwards; the festival went on to present its own productions of the piece in 1993, 2000 and 2005 – the latter (directed by John Cox, designed by Robert Perdziola and conducted by Douglas Boyd) reprised in its final season at its original address in 2010.

At the Metropolitan Opera in New York, where the opera had been introduced in 1894 (the company's tenth season), it was for decades an infrequent item in the repertory (no performances, for instance, were given between 1917 and 1940) until becoming a staple in the post-war era. Herbert Graf's 1940 staging, designed by Jonel Jorgulesco and conducted by Ettore Panizza, based on a close attention to manuscript additions to an original 1786 libretto housed in the Library of Congress, was significant in demonstrating to local audiences the emotional complexity hidden behind Mozart's apparently charming surface. Ezio Pinza, Licia Albanese, John Brownlee, Elisabeth Rethberg and Jarmila Novotná led a characteristically all-star cast. A 1998 staging by Jonathan Miller, designed by Peter J. Davison and conducted by James Levine, was the occasion for a public disagreement with a prima donna – Cecilia Bartoli, who was singing Susanna. Bartoli wanted to sing the replacement arietta and rondò Mozart composed for Adriana Ferrarese. Miller wanted her to stick to the originals. A compromise was finally reached whereby Bartoli sang the latter on the first night and her own preferences on the succeeding three. In *Opera*, Martin Bernheimer was unpersuaded by her Susanna, involving as it did 'a lot of rough, harsh tone, a great deal of robust and restless physical humour, endless mugging – vocal as well as facial – and unashamed vulgarity'; or, as Alex Ross put it more succinctly in the *New Yorker*, 'she tore around like a Disney character let loose in a Vermeer'.

If, from a musical point of view, productions of *Figaro* in recent decades have wandered back and forth between the poles of traditionalism (as exemplified, say, by Karajan, Böhm, Bernard Haitink, Riccardo Muti or Colin Davis) and the values of the historical performance movement (as represented by such figures as Arnold Östman, John Eliot Gardiner, Nikolaus Harnoncourt, René Jacobs or Marc Minkowski), stagings have tended either to remain firmly within the original eighteenth-century palatial setting – with David McVicar's move to 1830 in his Royal Opera House 2006 production effectively a sidestep rather than a rethinking of the piece – or to attempt to bring it up to date and much closer to home.

Highly influential among the latter type was Peter Sellars's staging set in an apartment designed by George Tsypin on the fifty-second floor of Trump Tower on New York's Fifth Avenue – part of a Mozart/Da Ponte trilogy developed at the (now defunct) PepsiCo Summerfare Festival held at Purchase, New York State, during the late 1980s. This *Figaro*, which opened in 1988, conducted by Craig Smith, delighted Mark Swed of the *Los Angeles Times*. 'As with all Sellars productions, the updating is dazzling, an outrageously entertaining spectacle, and one could fill pages detailing the director's seemingly limitless bag of titillating tricks [...] Here in a flamboyantly modern apartment, with [...] its prominent Frank Stella painting and avant-garde designer chairs, we have the Count as a business tycoon. Cherubino is a wonderfully gangly, sex-crazed teenager, who makes his entrance into Figaro's and Susanna's room (the laundry room, with a convertible sofa), noisily throwing down his hockey gear and heading straight for the fridge. Antonio, Mozart's and Da Ponte's gardener, is the surly, impossible building superintendent that all New York apartment dwellers know.'

And so on. Sellars's view of the piece was (largely) self-consistent as well as original, though Rodney Milnes's review in *Opera* noted a common (if often ignored) problem with updated productions – namely, that not all the elements within the revamped scenario actually fit the libretto. His other particularly pertinent comment pointed out that 'divorced from the context of European class structure, the character in James Maddalena's energetic reading [of the Count] became little more than a stupid thug'. Social class, for many commentators at all periods, has remained one of the essential elements of the opera's dramaturgical structure. Yet Sellars's opening of the door to contemporary settings – his staging was seen widely in Europe as well as released on video – proved seminal, and his justification would be echoed by many subsequent directors. 'That a system of contemporary references is an essential ingredient to the functioning of these pieces,' he wrote, 'seems relatively obvious.'

Christof Loy's 2001 Brussels staging (designed by Herbert Murauer and conducted by Antonio Pappano), however, compromised with a mixed-period approach evident in Herbert Murauer's costumes as part of a highly direct and physical production. Altogether more idiosyncratic was the Australian director Barrie Kosky's take on *Figaro* (sung in German) for the Komische Oper, Berlin, in 2005, designed by Klaus Grünberg and conducted by Kirill Petrenko. After the first two acts' blend of 'knockabout comedy, although with some genuinely clever updated "business"', yet with 'messy stagecraft' (as reported by *Opera*'s Barry Emslie), from the third act onwards the characters became Jewish (as is Kosky, and as was – by birth – Da Ponte). Thus 'we had a Jewish wedding, the men wore yarmulkas, the two girls in the duet were dressed as rabbis, [and] a bottle or glass was broken with cries of "Mazel tov!"' Emslie noted the 'extremely uncomfortable' audience reaction, though (in his words) 'the inevitable taboo clicked in, [curtailing] their disapproval of a production that many of them would have otherwise booed.'

Puzzlement, too, seems to have been the reaction of critic Michael Davidson to Jossi Wieler and Sergio Morabito's staging of *Figaro*, designed by Barbara Ehnes, in Amsterdam for the Mozart 250th anniversary season of 2006/07, when all three Mozart/Da Ponte operas were played on consecutive evenings. Davidson pointed out the crucial nature of class differences in the opera, here 'erased in the lame car-showroom setting [...] Cherubino became a mechanic and the Countess the flinty boss of the enterprise'. In the last act, 'tacky' film projections 'showed all sorts of sexual goings-on, whereas on stage one saw no interaction'. The conductor, Ingo Metzmacher, apparently insisted 'on valveless horns and "authentic bows"' while playing the continuo on a synthesizer. The production was, however, notable for presenting Danielle de Niese's first Susanna.

Salzburg offered performances of all of Mozart's operas during the anniversary year of 2006. New was Claus Guth's staging of *Figaro*, designed by Christian Schmidt, which, according to Richard Fairman, ran to nigh on four-and-a-half hours under Nikolaus Harnoncourt, whose conducting 'weighed down already slow tempos with extended pauses and a sledgehammer style that bangs every accent over the head'. Despite what he referred to as Guth's didacticism, Fairman praised the 'searching performances he drew out of his singers [...] here were theatrical performances to die for'; though he complained of the ubiquitous Cupid-like figure onstage for much of the opera manipulating events. An all-star cast included Bo Skovhus (Count), Dorothea Röschmann (Countess), Christine Schäfer (Cherubino), Anna Netrebko (Susanna) and Ildebrando D'Arcangelo (Figaro).

Back in Vienna, where it all started, Kaspar Bech Holten staged a 'cheeky, modern' *Figaro* at the Theater an der Wien in 2007, designed by Steffen Aarfing and conducted by Graeme Jenkins. 'Figaro is no servant,' explained reviewer Christopher Norton-Welsh in *Opera*, 'but the Count's manager and football teammate [...] Cherubino is the rising young star of the team, and is sold to another team as a punishment, Susanna is a make-up artist for the Countess, Basilio a cynical gossip journalist, and the chorus a crowd of paparazzi.' Despite this unusual relocation, 'Holten got excellent acting full of nuance from a highly satisfactory cast', who included Christopher Maltman (Count), Johan Reuter (Figaro), Andrea Rost (Countess), Elizabeth Futral (Susanna) and Anna Bonitatibus (Cherubino).

Where does *Figaro* go from here? It looks unlikely to lose its high repertory position any time soon. In a table of frequency of performance compiled by the website Operabase.com and analysing more than 100,000 performances of 2,156 works performed between the 2005/06 season and that of 2009/10, *Figaro* held fifth place. Mozart might be pleased to know that the Number 1 Spot was also his, with *Die Zauberflöte*, immediately followed by *La traviata*, *Carmen* and *La bohème*. Once regarded as a connoisseur's piece, felt to be too subtle and refined for wider public appeal, Mozart's complex comedy shows no signs of relinquishing its eventual and hard-won popularity.

Thematic Guide

Themes from the opera have been identified by the numbers in square brackets in the article on the music. These are also printed at corresponding points in the libretto, so that the words can be related to the musical themes.

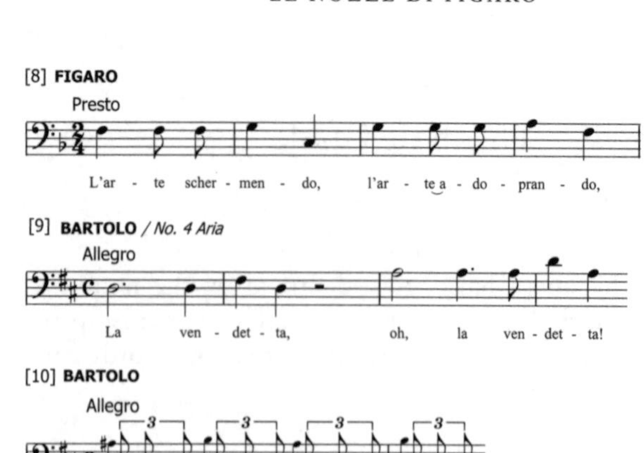
[8] FIGARO
Presto
L'ar - te scher - men - do, l'ar - te a - do - pran - do,
[9] BARTOLO / No. 4 Aria
Allegro
La ven - det - ta, oh, la ven - det - ta!
[10] BARTOLO
Allegro
Se tut - to il co - di - ce do - ves - si vol - ge - re,

[11] MARCELLINA / No. 5 Duet

Allegro
Via res - ti ser - vi - ta, ma - da - ma bril - lan - te.

[12] **CHERUBINO** / *No. 6 Aria*

Allegro vivace
Non so più co - sa son, co - sa fac - cio,

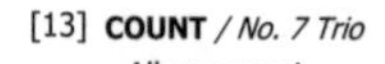
[13] COUNT / No. 7 Trio

Allegro assai
Co - sa sen - to! To - sto an - da - te,

[14] *No. 7 Trio*

[a] **BASILIO**

Allegro assai
In mal pun - to son qui giun - to;

[b] **SUSANNA**

Che ru - i - na, me me - schi - na,

[15] **PEASANTS** / *No. 8 Chorus*

Allegro
f p
Gio - va - ni lie - ti, fio - ri spar - ge - te

[16] **FIGARO** / *No. 9 Aria*

Vivace
Non più andrai, far - fal - lo - ne a - mo - ro - so,

[17] **FIGARO**

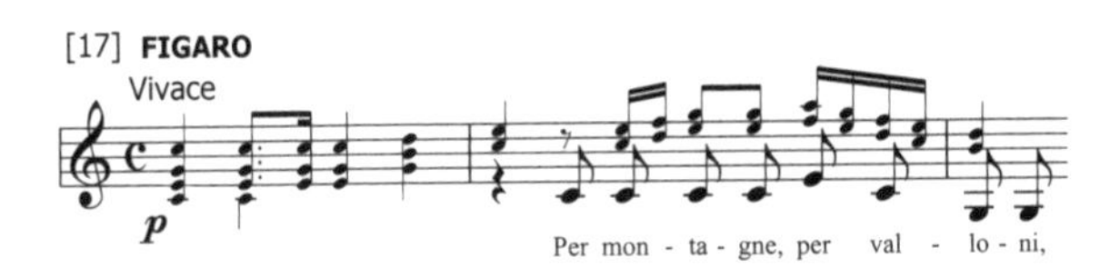
Vivace
p
Per mon - ta - gne, per val - lo - ni,

[18] **COUNTESS** / *No. 10 Cavatina*

Larghetto
Por - gi, a - mor, qual - che ri - sto - ro,

[19] **CHERUBINO** / *No. 11 Canzona*

Andante
Voi, che sa - pe - te che co - sa è a - mor,

[20] **SUSANNA** / *No. 12 Aria*

Allegretto
Ve - ni - te, in - gi - noc-chia - te - vi,

[21]

Allegretto
Se l'a - ma - no le fe - mi - ne, han cer - to il lor per - ché!

[22] **SUSANNA** / *No. 12a Arietta*

Allegro moderato
Un mo - to di gio - ia mi sen - to in pet - to,

[23] COUNT / No. 13 Trio
Allegro spirituoso
Su - san - na, or via sor - ti - te!
[24] SUSANNA / No. 14 Duet
Allegro assai
A - pri - te, presto a - pri - te, a - pri - te, è la Su - san - na,
[25] COUNT / No. 15 Finale
Allegro
E - sci o - mai, gar - zon mal - na - to;
[26]
COUNTESS Ah! la cie - ca ge - lo - si - a,
Allegro
COUNT Mo - ra, mo - ra!
[27] SUSANNA
Molto andante
Si - gno - re!
[28] FIGARO
Allegro
Si - gno - re, di fuo - ri son già i suo - na - to - ri,
[29] COUNT
Andante
Co - no - sce - te, si - gnor Fi - ga - ro, que - sto fo - glio chi ver - gò?
[30]
Andante

[31]
Allegro assai
MARCELLINA
f
Voi, si - gnor, che giu - sto sie - te,
BASILIO
BARTOLO

[32] COUNT / No. 16 Duet
Andante
Cru - del! per - ché fi - no - ra far - mi lan - guir co - sì?

[33] COUNT
Andante
p Mi sen - to dal con - ten - to

[34] COUNT / No. 17 Aria
Allegro maestoso
Ve - drò men - tr'io so - spi - ro, fe - li - ce un ser - vo mi - o!

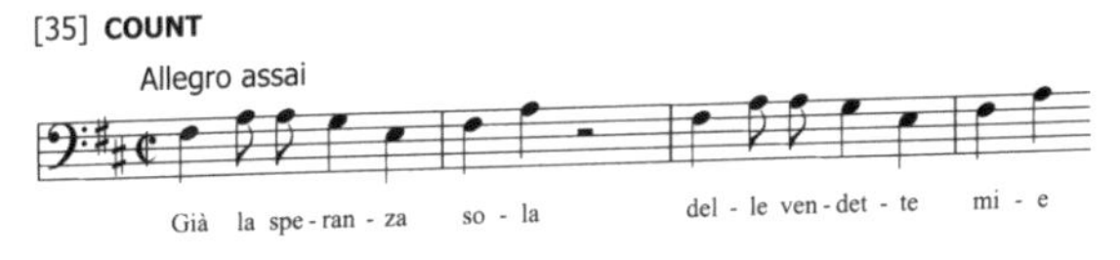
[35] COUNT
Allegro assai
Già la spe - ran - za so - la del - le ven - det - te mi - e

[36] MARCELLINA / No. 18 Sextet
Andante
Ri - co - no - sci in que - sto am - ples - so u - na ma - dre, a - ma - to fi - glio!

[37]
Andante
SUSANNA
Sua ma - dre?
BARTOLO
Sua ma - dre!
SUSANNA
Sua ma - dre?
COUNT
Sua ma - dre!
SUSANNA
Sua ma - dre?
CURZIO
Sua

ma - dre!
SUSANNA
Sua ma - dre!
MARCELLINA
Sua ma - dre!

[38] COUNTESS / No. 19 Aria
Andantino
p
Do - ve so - no i bei mo - men - ti,
[39] COUNTESS / from No. 20 Duet
Allegretto
p
Che so - a - ve zef - fi - ret - to,
[40] GIRLS / No. 21 Chorus
Grazioso
Ri - ce - ve - te, o pa - dron - ci - na,
[41] No. 22 Wedding March
Marcia
pp
[42] TWO GIRLS
Allegretto
A - man - ti co - stan - ti se - gua - ci d'o - nor,
[43] Fandango
Andante
tr
p
[44] BARBARINA / No. 23 Cavatina
Andante
L'ho per - du - ta, me me - schi - na! ah chi sa do - ve sa - rà,
[45] MARCELLINA / No. 24 Aria
Tempo di minuetto
Il ca - pro e la ca - pret - ta son sem - pre in a - mi - stà,
[46] MARCELLINA
Allegro
Sol noi po - ve - re fem - mi - ne, che tan - to a - miam quest' uo - mi - ni,

[47] **BASILIO** / *No. 25 Aria*

Andante
In quegli an - ni, in cui val po - co la mal pra - ti - ca ra - gion,

[48] **BASILIO**

Tempo di minuetto
Men - tre an - cor ta - ci - to guar - do quel do - no,

[49] **FIGARO** / *No. 26 Aria*

Moderato
A - pri - te un po' que gli oc - chi, uo - mi - ni in - cau - ti e scioc - chi.

[50] **SUSANNA** / *No. 27 Aria*

Andante
p
Deh, vie - ni, non tar - dar, o gio - ia bel - la.

[51] **SUSANNA** / *No. 27a Rondò*

Al de - si - o di chi t'a - do - ra, vie - ni, vo - la, o mia spe - ran - za!

[52] **CHERUBINO** / *No. 28 Finale*

Andante
f p 3 sfp
Pian, pia - nin le an - dro più pres - so,

[53] **FIGARO**

Larghetto
Tut - to è tran - quil - lo e pla - ci - do,

[54] **SUSANNA**

Allegro molto
Ehi Fi - ga - ro! ta - ce - te!
sfp sfp sfp

[55] **FIGARO**

Andante

[56] **COUNT**

Allegro assai

[57] **COUNT**

[58] **TUTTI**

Allegro assai

Le nozze di Figaro

Note on the Text

Julian Rushton

The ordering of scenes in Act Three departs from the sequence of scenes in Beaumarchais and may appear somewhat arbitrary. In 1965 R.B. Moberly and Christopher Raeburn suggested that scenes five to eight were rearranged at a late stage by Mozart and Da Ponte. They suggested a revised order for scenes five to eight, following the Count's *scena* 'Hai già vinta la causa' and the aria 'Vedrò, mentre io sospiro'.[1]

TRADITIONAL ORDER	MOBERLY/RAEBURN ORDER
Scene five recit.: 'È decisa la lite'; sextet 'Riconosci in questo amplesso' (Count and Curzio exit)	Scene five recit.: Barbarina, Cherubino 'Andiam, andiam bel paggio'
Scene six recit.: 'Eccovi, oh caro amico'	Scene six *scena* (Countess): 'E Susanna non vien'; aria: 'Dove sono i bei momenti'
Scene seven recit.: Barbarina, Cherubino (Andiam, andiam bel paggio)*	Scene seven recit.: 'È decisa la lite'; sextet 'Riconosci in questo amplesso' (Count and Curzio exit)
Scene eight *scena* (Countess): 'E Susanna non vien'; aria: 'Dove sono i bei momenti'	Scene eight recit.: 'Eccovi, oh caro amico'

The versions unite for scene nine, the entry of Antonio (recit.: 'Io vi dico, signor'). This order can be performed only if Bartolo and

1 R.B. Moberly and Christopher Raeburn, 'Mozart's "Figaro": The Plan of Act III', in *Music & Letters,* 46 (1965), pp. 134–36.

Antonio are taken by different singers, as there is no time available to change costume from doctor to gardener, and this provides a motive for the alleged reordering.

The Moberly-Raeburn suggestion has considerable merits:

a. It permits the Count to leave the stage, as is normal following a *scena* with recitative and aria.
b. In the traditional order, Cherubino and Barbarina leave the stage and Antonio appears immediately to report that the page's clothes have been found in his cottage.
c. Figaro is involved in the short scene three; Susanna says 'you've won your case' ('hai già vinta la causa'), precipitating the Count's *scena*. But there is no time for a trial to take place before scene five, in which Figaro's parentage is revealed. Moving the Countess's *scena* to this point allows time for a brief trial off stage.
d. In scene six Susanna hands Figaro her dowry, money that came from the Countess. She would surely go to the Countess after 'Eccovi, oh caro amico' to report these developments, but the Countess appears and complains that she has not come: 'E Susanna non vien'.
e. The Countess's *scena* is better placed before the outcome of the trial is known. This sequence is less confusing for the audience, and it juxtaposes the two grand soliloquies for the nobility, mirroring the juxtaposition of soliloquies for the servant couple in Act Four.

A number of conductors, following the lead of Charles Mackerras with English National Opera, have adopted the revised order, although it requires an additional singer for Antonio. Moberly and Raeburn tried to support their theory by reference to the keys of the various numbers, superficially more logical in their ordering, but such key-schemes, however seductive on paper, fail to take into account the transition of keys affected by recitative; the keys of the main numbers are not juxtaposed and Mozart's practice in this opera and elsewhere (for instance in *Don Giovanni*) suggest that an apparently rational order of keys came low at best among his priorities. And if Mozart had planned his key-scheme, it would have included the key of the short aria for Cherubino included in the first printed libretto (at * in the table above), but omitted from the score (no music survives to tell us what key would have been used).

The earliest musical source offers no support for the revised ordering, while not absolutely ruling it out. This is made clear in Alan Tyson's careful study of the autograph.[2] Mozart did not compose his operas in a steady sequence from beginning to end. Recitatives were nearly always composed last, so that the fact that in the autograph scene six ends and scene seven (traditional order) begins on the same page does not completely destroy the Moberly-Raeburn theory.

2 Alan Tyson, '*Le nozze di Figaro*: Lessons from the Autograph Score', first published in 1981 and reprinted in *Mozart: Studies of the Autograph Scores* (Cambridge, MA: Harvard University Press, 1987, pp. 114–124).

THE CHARACTERS

COUNT ALMAVIVA, *a Spanish nobleman*	baritone
COUNTESS ALMAVIVA, *his wife*	soprano
SUSANNA, *the Countess's maid, promised in marriage to*	soprano
FIGARO, *the Count's man-servant*	bass
CHERUBINO, *the Count's page*	soprano
MARCELLINA, *a housekeeper*	soprano
DOCTOR BARTOLO, *a doctor of Seville*	bass
DON BASILIO, *a music teacher*	tenor
DON CURZIO, *a lawyer*	tenor
BARBARINA, *daughter of*	soprano
ANTONIO, *a gardener and Susanna's uncle*	bass
TWO SERVANT GIRLS	sopranos

Chorus of countrymen and countrywomen

Aguas Frescas, near Seville, the Almavivas' country house

Le nozze di Figaro

Opera buffa in Four Acts
by Wolfgang Amadeus Mozart (K492)

Libretto by Lorenzo Da Ponte
after the play *La Folle Journée, ou Le Mariage de Figaro*
by Pierre-Augustin Caron de Beaumarchais

English translation by Opernführer

Translation of Susanna's alternative aria
and rondo by Charles Johnston

Le nozze di Figaro was first performed at the Burgtheater, Vienna, on 1st May 1786. It was first performed in Britain at the King's Theatre, Haymarket, on 18th June 1812. The first performance in the United States was at the Park Theatre, New York, on 10th May 1824 (in English).

For the 1789 revival in Vienna, Mozart revised the score to accommodate the particular vocal abilities of Lorenzo Da Ponte's mistress Adriana Ferrarese (later to sing the first Fiordiligi in *Così fan tutte*) as Susanna. The arietta 'Un moto di gioia' replaced 'Venite, inginocchiatevi' in Act Two and the rondò 'Al desio di chi t'adora' replaced 'Deh vieni, non tardar' in Act Four.

Ouvertura [1,2,3]

ATTO PRIMO

Scena I

Camera non affatto ammobiliata, una sedia d'appoggio in mezzo.

Figaro con una misura in mano e Susanna allo specchio che si sta mettendo un cappellino ornato di fiori.

N°1 Duettino

FIGARO *(misurando)*
Cinque… dieci… venti… trenta… [4]
trentasei… quarantatré…

SUSANNA *(fra sé stessa, guardandosi nello specchio)*
Ora sì ch'io son contenta; [5]
sembra fatto inver per me.
Guarda un po', mio caro Figaro,
guarda adesso il mio cappello.

FIGARO
Sì mio core, or è più bello,
sembra fatto inver per te.

SUSANNA e FIGARO
Ah, il mattino alle nozze vicino
quanto è dolce al mio (tuo) tenero sposo
questo bel cappellino vezzoso
che Susanna ella stessa si fe'.

Recitativo

SUSANNA
Cosa stai misurando,
caro il mio Figaretto?

Overture [1,2,3]

ACT ONE

Scene I

A partly furnished room, with an easy chair in the centre.

Figaro with a measure in his hand, Susanna at the mirror, trying on a hat decorated with flowers.

No. 1 Duet

FIGARO *(measuring the room)*
Five… ten… twenty… thirty… [4]
thirty-six… forty-three…

SUSANNA *(to herself, gazing into the mirror)*
Yes, I'm very pleased with that; [5]
it seems just made for me.
Take a look, dear Figaro,
just look at this hat of mine.

FIGARO
Yes, my dearest, it's very pretty;
it looks just made for you.

SUSANNA and FIGARO
On this morning of our wedding
how delightful to my (your) dear one
is this pretty little hat
which Susanna made herself.

Recitative

SUSANNA
What are you measuring,
my dearest Figaro?

FIGARO
Io guardo se quel letto
che ci destina il Conte
farà buona figura in questo loco.

SUSANNA
E in questa stanza?

FIGARO
Certo: a noi la cede
generoso il padrone.

SUSANNA
Io per me te la dono.

FIGARO
E la ragione?

SUSANNA *(toccandosi la fronte)*
La ragione l'ho qui.

FIGARO *(facendo lo stesso)*
Perché non puoi
far che passi un po' qui?

SUSANNA
Perché non voglio.
Sei tu mio servo o no?

FIGARO
Ma non capisco
perché tanto ti spiace
la più comoda stanza del palazzo.

SUSANNA
Perch'io son la Susanna, e tu sei pazzo.

FIGARO
Grazie; non tanti elogi! Guarda un poco
se potriasi star meglio in altro loco.

N°2 Duettino

FIGARO
Se a caso madama [6]
la notte ti chiama,

FIGARO
I'm seeing if this bed
which the Count has put aside for us
will go well just here.

SUSANNA
In this room?

FIGARO
Of course: his lordship's
generously giving it to us.

SUSANNA
As far as I'm concerned, you can keep it.

FIGARO
What's the matter?

SUSANNA *(tapping her forehead)*
I've my reasons in here.

FIGARO *(doing the same)*
Why can't you
let me in on them?

SUSANNA
Because I don't choose to.
Are you my servant or not?

FIGARO
But I don't understand
why you so dislike
the most convenient room in the palace.

SUSANNA
Because I'm Susanna and you're a dolt.

FIGARO
Thanks, you're too flattering: just see
if it could go better anywhere else.

No. 2 Duet

FIGARO
Supposing my lady [6]
calls you at night –

din din: in due passi
da quella puoi gir.
Vien poi l'occasione
che vuolmi il padrone,
don, don: in tre salti
lo vado a servir.

SUSANNA
Così se il mattino
il caro Contino,
din din, e ti manda
tre miglia lontan,
don don, a mia porta
il diavol lo porta,
ed ecco in tre salti…

FIGARO
Susanna, pian, pian.

SUSANNA
Ascolta…

FIGARO
Fa' presto…

SUSANNA
Se udir brami il resto,
discaccia i sospetti
che torto mi fan.

FIGARO
Udir bramo il resto,
i dubbi, i sospetti
gelare mi fan.

Recitativo

SUSANNA
Or bene, ascolta e taci!

FIGARO *(inquieto)*
Parla: che c'è di nuovo?

ding ding: in two steps
you can be there from here.
Or if it should happen
that his lordship should want me,
dong dong: in three bounds
I'm there at his service.

SUSANNA
And supposing one morning
the dear Count should ring,
ding ding, and send you
three miles away,
dong dong, and the devil
should lead him to my door?
Dong dong, in three bounds…

FIGARO
Hush, hush, Susanna.

SUSANNA
Listen.

FIGARO
Quick, tell me!

SUSANNA
If you wish to hear the rest,
banish those suspicions
which do me wrong.

FIGARO
I burn to hear the rest:
doubts and suspicions
freeze my blood.

Recitative

SUSANNA
Well then, listen and keep quiet.

FIGARO *(nervously)*
Speak: what's there to tell?

SUSANNA

Il signor Conte,
stanco di andar cacciando le straniere
bellezze forestiere,
vuole ancor nel castello
ritentar la sua sorte,
né già di sua consorte, bada bene,
appetito gli viene…

FIGARO

E di chi dunque?

SUSANNA

Della tua Susannetta

FIGARO *(con sorpresa)*

Di te?

SUSANNA

Di me medesma; ed ha speranza,
che al nobil suo progetto
utilissima sia tal vicinanza.

FIGARO

Bravo! Tiriamo avanti.

SUSANNA

Queste le grazie son, questa la cura
ch'egli prende di te, della tua sposa.

FIGARO

Oh, guarda un po', che carità pelosa!

SUSANNA

Chètati, or viene il meglio: Don Basilio,
mio maestro di canto e suo mezzano,
nel darmi la lezione
mi ripete ogni dì questa canzone.

FIGARO

Chi? Basilio? Oh birbante!

SUSANNA

The noble Count,

tired of scouring the countryside
for fresh beauties,
wants to try his luck again
in his own palace –
though, let me tell you, it's not his wife
who whets his appetite.

FIGARO

Well, who then?

SUSANNA

Your little Susanna.

FIGARO *(surprised)*

You?

SUSANNA

The very same, and he's hoping
that being so close will be most useful
to his noble project.

FIGARO

Bravo! Go on.

SUSANNA

This is the gracious favour, this the care
he bestows on you and on your wife.

FIGARO

Have you seen such condescension!

SUSANNA

Wait though: there's better to come.
Don Basilio, my singing teacher and his
factotum, repeats this same theme daily
when he gives me my lesson.

FIGARO

What, Basilio? The scoundrel!

SUSANNA

E tu credevi
che fosse la mia dote
merto del tuo bel muso!

FIGARO
Me n'ero lusingato.

SUSANNA

Ei la destina
per ottener da me certe mezz'ore…
che il diritto feudale…

FIGARO
Come? Ne' feudi suoi
non l'ha il Conte abolito?

SUSANNA
Ebben; ora è pentito, e par che tenti
Riscattarlo da me.

FIGARO

Bravo! Mi piace:
che caro signor Conte!
Ci vogliam divertir: trovato avete…

(Si sente suonare un campanello.)

Chi suona? La Contessa.

SUSANNA
Addio, addio, addio, Figaro bello…

FIGARO
Coraggio, mio tesoro.

SUSANNA

E tu, cervello.

(parte)

SUSANNA

Did you imagine

he gave me a dowry
for the sake of your *beaux yeux*?

FIGARO

So I'd flattered myself.

SUSANNA

He intends it

to obtain from me certain half-hours…
which feudal privilege…

FIGARO

What! Didn't the Count
abolish that in his domain?

SUSANNA

He did, but now regrets it; and it seems
he wants to bring it back for me.

FIGARO

Well! Very pretty:

how charming of his lordship!
He wants some fun: he'll get it…

(A bell rings.)

Who's ringing? The Countess.

SUSANNA

Goodbye, goodbye, goodbye Figaro, my dear.

FIGARO

Courage, my dearest.

SUSANNA

And you be wary.

(exit)

Scena II

Figaro solo.

FIGARO *(passeggiando con fuoco per la camera, e fregandosi le mani)*
Bravo, signor padrone! Ora incomincio
a capir il mistero... e a veder schietto
tutto il vostro progetto: a Londra è vero?
Voi ministro, io corriero, e la Susanna...
secreta ambasciatrice...
Non sarà, non sarà, Figaro il dice.

N°3 Cavatina

FIGARO
Se vuol ballare, [7]
signor Contino,
il chitarrino
le suonerò.
Se vuol venire
nella mia scuola
la capriola
le insegnerò.
Saprò... ma piano,
meglio ogni arcano
dissimulando
scoprir potrò!
L'arte schermendo, [8]
l'arte adoprando,
di qua pungendo,
di là scherzando,
tutte le macchine
rovescerò.
Se vuol ballare,
signor Contino,
il chitarrino
le suonerò.

(parte)

Scene II

Figaro alone.

FIGARO *(feverishly pacing up and down the room, rubbing his hands)*
Well done, my noble master! Now I begin
to understand the secret… and to see
your whole scheme clearly: to London, isn't it?
You go as minister, I as courier, and Susanna…
confidential attachée…
It shall not be: Figaro has said it.

No. 3 Cavatina

FIGARO
If, my dear Count, [7]
you feel like dancing,
it's I
who'll call the tune.
If you'll come
to my school,
I'll teach you
how to caper.
I'll know how… but wait,
I can uncover
his secret design
more easily by dissembling.
Acting stealthily, [8]
acting openly,
here stinging,
there mocking,
all your plots
I'll overthrow.
If, my dear Count,
you feel like dancing,
it's I
who'll call the tune.

(exit)

Scena III

Bartolo e Marcellina con un contratto in mano.

Recitativo

BARTOLO
Ed aspettaste il giorno
fissato a le sue nozze
per parlarmi di questo?

MARCELLINA
Io non mi perdo,
dottor mio, di coraggio:
per romper de' sponsali
più avanzati di questo
bastò spesso un pretesto, ed egli ha meco,
oltre questo contratto, certi impegni…
so io… basta… convien
la Susanna atterrir. Convien con arte
impuntigliarli a rifiutar il Conte.
Egli per vendicarsi
prenderà il mio partito,
e Figaro così fia mio marito.

BARTOLO *(prende il contratto dalle mani di Marcellina)*
Bene, io tutto farò: senza riserve
tutto a me palesate.

(tra sé)

Avrei pur gusto
di dar per moglie la mia serva antica
a chi mi fece un dì rapir l'amica.

N°4 *Aria*

BARTOLO
La vendetta, oh, la vendetta! [9]
È un piacer serbato ai saggi.
L'obliar l'onte e gli oltraggi
è bassezza, è ognor viltà.

Scene III

Enter Bartolo and Marcellina with a contract in her hand.

Recitative

BARTOLO
And you waited until the day
appointed for his wedding
to tell me this?

MARCELLINA
Oh, my dear doctor,
I'm not giving up:
to break off engagements
even later than this
a pretext has often sufficed, and besides
this contract he has certain pledges to me
I could mention... but enough; now
we must frighten Susanna. We must somehow
make her reject the Count's advances.
To revenge himself,
he'll take my part,
and so Figaro will become my husband.

BARTOLO *(taking the contract from Marcellina's hand)*
Well, I'll do all I can; without reserve
tell me everything.

(aside)

I'd enjoy
giving him my old servant for a wife
for having stolen my intended from me.

No. 4 Aria

BARTOLO
Revenge, yes, revenge [9]
is a pleasure meant for the intelligent;
to forget insults and outrages
is always low and base.

Con l'astuzia... coll'arguzia...
col giudizio... col criterio...
si potrebbe... il fatto è serio...
ma credete si farà.
Se tutto il codice [10]
dovessi volgere,
se tutto l'indice
dovessi leggere,
con un equivoco,
con un sinonimo
qualche garbuglio
si troverà.
Tutta Siviglia
conosce Bartolo:
il birbo Figaro
vostro sarà.

(parte)

Scena IV

Marcellina, poi Susanna, con cuffia da donna, un nastro ed un abito da donna.

Recitativo

MARCELLINA
Tutto ancor non ho perso:
mi resta la speranza.
Ma Susanna si avanza:
io vo' provarmi...
Fingiam di non vederla.

(tra sé, forte)

E quella buona perla
la vorrebbe sposar!

SUSANNA *(resta indietro, tra sé)*
Di me favella.

With astuteness and acuteness,
with judgement and discernment,
I can do it... The case is serious...
but, believe me, I'll bring it off.
If I have to search [10]
the whole legal code,
if I have to read through
the whole statute book,
with a quibble
or a paraphrase
I'll find
some obstacle.
All Seville
knows Dr Bartolo:
that rascal Figaro
will be yours!

(exit)

Scene IV

Marcellina, then Susanna, carrying a lady's cap, a ribbon, and a dress.

Recitative

MARCELLINA
All is not lost yet;
I still have hopes.
But here comes Susanna:
I'll make a start.
Let's pretend not to see her.

(aside, loudly)

And that's the pearl of virtue
he intends to marry!

SUSANNA *(holding back, aside)*
She's talking of me.

MARCELLINA
Ma da Figaro alfine
non può meglio sperarsi: *argent fait tout.*

SUSANNA *(tra sé)*
Che lingua! Manco male
ch'ognun sa quanto vale.

MARCELLINA
Brava! Questo è giudizio!
Con quegli occhi modesti,
con quell'aria pietosa,
e poi…

SUSANNA *(tra sé)*
Meglio è partir.

MARCELLINA *(tra sé)*
Che cara sposa!

N°5 *Duettino*

MARCELLINA *(facendo una riverenza)*
Via resti servita, [11]
madama brillante.

SUSANNA *(facendo una riverenza)*
Non sono sì ardita,
madama piccante.

MARCELLINA *(facendo una riverenza)*
No, prima a lei tocca.

SUSANNA *(facendo una riverenza)*
No, no, tocca a lei.

SUSANNA e MARCELLINA *(facendo una riverenza)*
Io so i dover miei,
non fo inciviltà.

MARCELLINA *(facendo una riverenza)*
La sposa novella!

MARCELLINA
But, after all, from Figaro
one can't hope for anything better: *argent fait tout.*

SUSANNA *(aside)*
How sophisticated! It's lucky
everyone knows the worth of what she says.

MARCELLINA
Bravo! such discretion!
And those modest eyes
and demure expression,
as well as...

SUSANNA *(aside)*
I'd better go.

MARCELLINA *(aside)*
What a charming bride!

No. 5 Duet

MARCELLINA *(making a curtsey)*
After you, [11]
gracious lady.

SUSANNA *(making a curtsey)*
I'd not be so bold,
worthy ma'am.

MARCELLINA *(making a curtsey)*
No, you go first, pray.

SUSANNA *(making a curtsey)*
No, no, after you.

SUSANNA and MARCELLINA *(making a curtsey)*
I know my place,
I'd not so presume.

MARCELLINA *(making a curtsey)*
A bride-to-be first.

SUSANNA *(facendo una riverenza)*
La dama d'onore!

MARCELLINA *(facendo una riverenza)*
Del Conte la bella!

SUSANNA *(facendo una riverenza)*
Di Spagna l'amore!

MARCELLINA
I meriti!

SUSANNA
L'abito!

MARCELLINA
Il posto!

SUSANNA
L'età!

MARCELLINA *(infuriata)*
Per Bacco, precipito,
se ancor resto qua.

SUSANNA
Sibilla decrepita,
da rider mi fa.

(Marcellina parte infuriata.)

Scena V

Susanna, e poi Cherubino.

Recitativo

SUSANNA
Va' là, vecchia pedante,
dottoressa arrogante,
perché hai letto due libri
e seccata madama in gioventù...

SUSANNA *(making a curtsey)*
A lady in waiting.

MARCELLINA *(making a curtsey)*
The Count's favourite.

SUSANNA *(making a curtsey)*
The toast of Spain.

MARCELLINA
Your qualities.

SUSANNA
Your dress.

MARCELLINA
Your position.

SUSANNA
Your age.

MARCELLINA *(enraged)*
I'll fly into a rage
if I stay here any longer.

SUSANNA
Decrepit old witch,
she's a laughing-stock.

(exit Marcellina in a fury)

Scene V

Susanna, then Cherubino.

Recitative

SUSANNA
Get away, you old frump!
Putting on high and mighty airs
because you've read a couple of books
and used to torment my lady in her youth...

CHERUBINO *(esce in fretta)*
Susannetta, sei tu?

SUSANNA
Son io, cosa volete?

CHERUBINO
Ah, cor mio, che accidente!

SUSANNA
Cor vostro! Cosa avvenne?

CHERUBINO
Il Conte ieri,
perché trovommi sol con Barbarina,
il congedo mi diede;
e se la Contessina,
la mia bella comare,
grazia non m'intercede, io vado via,

(con ansietà)

io non ti vedo più, Susanna mia!

SUSANNA
Non vedete più me! Bravo! Ma dunque
non più per la Contessa
secretamente il vostro cor sospira?

CHERUBINO
Ah, che troppo rispetto ella m'ispira!
Felice te, che puoi
vederla quando vuoi,
che la vesti il mattino,
che la sera la spogli, che le metti
gli spilloni, i merletti...

(con un sospiro)

Ah, se in tuo loco...
Cos'hai lì? Dimmi un poco...

CHERUBINO *(entering hurriedly)*
Susanna dear, is it you?

SUSANNA
Yes, it's me. What do you want?

CHERUBINO
Oh my dearest, what a misfortune!

SUSANNA
Your dearest! What's happened?

CHERUBINO
Yesterday the Count,
because he found me all alone
with Barbarina, dismissed me:
and if the Countess,
my lovely godmother, doesn't intercede
to get me pardoned, I'll have to go away

(anxiously)

and never see my dear Susanna again!

SUSANNA
Never see me again! Well then!
But isn't your heart secretly sighing
any longer for the Countess?

CHERUBINO
Ah, she fills me with too much respect!
How lucky you are, to be able
to see her whenever you wish!
You dress her in the morning
and undress her at night; you fix
her pins, her laces...

(sighing)

If only I could be in your place...
What have you got there? Let me see...

SUSANNA *(imitandolo)*
Ah, il vago nastro e la notturna cuffia
di comare sì bella...

CHERUBINO
Deh, dammelo sorella,
dammelo per pietà!

(Cherubino toglie il nastro di mano a Susanna.)

SUSANNA *(vuol riprenderglielo)*
Presto quel nastro!

CHERUBINO *(si mette a girare intorno alla sedia)*
O caro, o bello, o fortunato nastro!
Io non te'l renderò che colla vita!

(Bacia e ribacia il nastro.)

SUSANNA *(seguita a corrergli dietro, ma poi si arresta come fosse stanca)*
Cos'è quest'insolenza?

CHERUBINO
Eh via, sta' cheta!
In ricompensa poi
questa mia canzonetta io ti vo' dare.

SUSANNA
E che ne debbo fare?

CHERUBINO
Leggila alla padrona,
leggila tu medesma;
leggila a Barbarina, a Marcellina;

(con trasporto di gioia)

leggila ad ogni donna del palazzo!

SUSANNA
Povero Cherubin, siete voi pazzo?

SUSANNA *(imitating him)*
Oh what a pretty ribbon, and the nightcap
of so lovely a godmother...

CHERUBINO
Oh give me it, my dear.
Give me it, I beg.

(He snatches the ribbon from her hand.)

SUSANNA *(trying to take it back)*
Give it back at once.

CHERUBINO *(dodging round the easy chair)*
O dear, sweet, fortunate ribbon!
I'll not give it up except with my life.

(He kisses the ribbon again and again.)

SUSANNA *(beginning to run after him, but then stopping as if tired)*
What is this insolence?

CHERUBINO
Go on, don't be angry!
In exchange for it I'll give you
this little song of mine.

SUSANNA
And what am I to do with it?

CHERUBINO
Read it to my lady,
read it for yourself,
read it to Barbarina, Marcellina,

(with joy)

read it to every woman in the palace.

SUSANNA
Poor Cherubino, have you gone mad?

N°6 Aria

CHERUBINO
Non so più cosa son, cosa faccio, [12]
or di foco, ora sono di ghiaccio,
ogni donna cangiar di colore,
ogni donna mi fa palpitar.
Solo ai nomi d'amor, di diletto,
mi si turba, mi s'altera il petto
e a parlare mi sforza d'amore
un desio ch'io non posso spiegar.
Parlo d'amor vegliando,
parlo d'amor sognando,
all'acque, all'ombre, ai monti,
ai fiori, all'erbe, ai fonti,
all'eco, all'aria, ai venti,
che il suon de' vani accenti
portano via con sé.
E se non ho chi mi oda,
parlo d'amor con me.

Scena VI

Cherubino, Susanna e poi il Conte.

Recitativo

CHERUBINO
Ah, son perduto!

(Cherubino vedendo il Conte da lontano, torna indietro impaurito e si nasconde dietro la sedia.)

SUSANNA
Che timor… Il Conte!

(Susanna cerca mascherar Cherubino.)

Misera me!

No. 6 Aria

CHERUBINO

I no longer know what I am or what I'm doing, [12]
now I'm burning, now I'm made of ice;
every woman makes me change colour,
every woman makes me tremble.
At the very word 'love' or 'beloved'
my heart leaps and pounds,
and to speak of it fills me
with a longing I can't explain!
I speak of love when I'm awake,
I speak of it in my dreams,
to the stream, the shade, the mountains,
to the flowers, the grass, the springs,
to the echo, the air, the breezes,
which carry away with them
the sound of my fond words…
And if I've none to hear me,
I speak of love to myself.

Scene VI

Cherubino, Susanna, then the Count.

Recitative

CHERUBINO

Ah, I'm lost!

(Cherubino, seeing the Count approaching, doubles back in fright and hides behind the easy chair.)

SUSANNA

Heavens… The Count!

(She tries to conceal Cherubino.)

Woe is me!

IL CONTE *(entrando)*
Susanna, tu mi sembri
agitata e confusa.

SUSANNA
Signor… io chiedo scusa…
ma… se mai… qui sorpresa…
per carità! Partite.

IL CONTE *(si mette a sedere sulla sedia, prende Susanna per la mano: ella si distacca con forza)*
Un momento, e ti lascio.
Odi.

SUSANNA
Non odo nulla.

IL CONTE
Due parole. Tu sai
che ambasciatore a Londra
il re mi dichiarò; di condur meco
Figaro destinai.

SUSANNA *(timida)*
Signor, se osassi…

IL CONTE *(alzandosi)*
Parla, parla, mia cara, e con quel dritto
ch'oggi prendi su me finché tu vivi
chiedi, imponi, prescrivi.

(con tenerezza, e tentando riprenderle la mano)

SUSANNA
Lasciatemi signor; dritti non prendo,
non ne vo', non ne intendo… oh me infelice!

IL CONTE
Ah no, Susanna, io ti vo' far felice!
Tu ben sai quanto io t'amo: a te Basilio

COUNT *(entering)*
Susanna, you seem to be
agitated and confused.

SUSANNA
My lord… pray excuse me…
but… suppose someone caught us…
I beg you to leave.

COUNT *(He seats himself in the easy-chair and takes Susanna's hand, which she withdraws with an effort)*
One moment and I'll leave you.
Listen.

SUSANNA
I mustn't listen.

COUNT
Just two words. You know
that the king has appointed me
ambassador in London: I planned
to take Figaro with me.

SUSANNA *(shyly)*
My lord, if you'd allow me…

COUNT *(rising)*
Speak, speak, my dear, and with that right
which today you may assume of me as long as you live,
ask, require, demand.

(tenderly, trying to take her hand again)

SUSANNA
Let me go, my lord; I claim no right,
nor wish, nor intend to… I'm so unhappy!

COUNT
But no, Susanna, I want to make you happy!
You well know how much I love you:

tutto già disse. Or senti,
se per pochi momenti
meco in giardin sull'imbrunir del giorno...
ah, per questo favore io pagherei...

BASILIO *(dentro le quinte)*
È uscito poco fa.

IL CONTE
Chi parla?

SUSANNA
Oh Dei!

IL CONTE
Esci, e alcun non entri.

SUSANNA
Ch'io vi lasci qui solo?

BASILIO *(come sopra)*
Da madama ei sarà, vado a cercarlo.

IL CONTE *(addita la sedia)*
Qui dietro mi porrò.

SUSANNA
Non vi celate.

IL CONTE
Taci, e cerca ch'ei parta.

(Il Conte vuol nascondersi dietro il sedile: Susanna si frappone tra il paggio e lui. Il Conte la spinge dolcemente. Ella rincula; intanto il paggio passa al davanti del sedile, si mette dentro in piedi. Susanna il ricopre colla vestaglia.)

SUSANNA
Oimè! Che fate?

Basilio has already told you; now listen.
If you'll give me a few minutes
in the garden at dusk...
for that favour, ah, I'd pay...

BASILIO *(offstage)*
He's just gone out.

COUNT
Who spoke?

SUSANNA
Oh, Heavens!

COUNT
Go out, and see no one comes in.

SUSANNA
I'm to leave you here alone?

BASILIO *(as above)*
He'll be with my lady: I'll go and look for him.

COUNT *(indicating the easy chair)*
I'll get behind here.

SUSANNA
Do not hide there.

COUNT
Hush, and get rid of him.

(The Count goes to hide behind the chair: Susanna interposes herself between the page and him. The Count pushes her gently aside. She withdraws; the page steals in front of the chair and curls up inside it. Susanna covers him with the dress.)

SUSANNA
Alas! What are you doing?

Scena VII

Susanna, il Conte, Cherubino, Basilio

BASILIO *(entrando)*
Susanna, il ciel vi salvi. Avreste a caso
veduto il Conte?

SUSANNA
E cosa
deve far meco il Conte? Animo, uscite.

BASILIO
Aspettate, sentite,
Figaro di lui cerca.

SUSANNA *(tra sé)*
Oh cielo!

(forte)

Ei cerca
chi dopo voi più l'odia.

IL CONTE *(tra sé)*
Veggiam come mi serve.

BASILIO
Io non ho mai nella moral sentito
ch'uno ch'ami la moglie odi il marito.
Per dir che il Conte v'ama…

SUSANNA *(con risentimento)*
Sortite, vil ministro
dell'altrui sfrenatezza: io non ho d'uopo
della vostra morale,
del Conte, del suo amor…

BASILIO
Non c'è alcun male.
Ha ciascun i suoi gusti: io mi credea
che preferir dovreste per amante,
come fan tutte quante,

Scene VII

Susanna, the Count, Cherubino, Basilio.

BASILIO *(entering)*
Susanna, Heaven be with you. Have you by any chance
seen the Count?

SUSANNA
What should the Count be doing here
with me? Please go away.

BASILIO
Just a moment, listen;
Figaro's looking for him.

SUSANNA *(aside)*
Oh Heaven!

(aloud)

He's looking for the one
who, after you, hates him most.

COUNT *(aside)*
We'll see how I am served.

BASILIO
I've never heard the proposition
that one who loves the wife must hate the husband.
To tell you how the Count loves you…

SUSANNA *(reproachfully)*
Begone, base agent
for another's lust: I don't need
your propositions,
your Count and his love…

BASILIO
There's no harm done: everyone
to his own taste: I'd have thought
that for a lover you'd prefer,
like any other woman,

un signor liberal, prudente, e saggio,
a un giovinastro, a un paggio...

SUSANNA *(con ansietà)*

A Cherubino!

BASILIO

A Cherubino! A Cherubin d'amore
ch'oggi sul far del giorno
passeggiava qui intorno,
per entrar...

SUSANNA *(con forza)*

Uom maligno,
un'impostura è questa.

BASILIO

È un maligno con voi chi ha gli occhi in testa.
E quella canzonetta?
Ditemi in confidenza; io sono amico,
ed altrui nulla dico;
è per voi, per madama...

SUSANNA *(mostra dello smarrimento, tra sé)*

Chi diavol gliel'ha detto?

BASILIO

A proposito, figlia,
instruitelo meglio; egli la guarda
a tavola sì spesso,
e con tale immodestia,
che se il Conte s'accorge... e su tal punto,
sapete, egli è una bestia.

SUSANNA

Scellerato!
E perché andate voi
tai menzogne spargendo?

a generous, prudent and discreet nobleman
to a youngster, a pageboy...

SUSANNA *(anxiously)*
To Cherubino?

BASILIO
To Cherubino, that amorous cherub
who at daybreak this morning
was prowling about here
trying to get in...

SUSANNA *(loud)*
Slanderer!
It's an invention!

BASILIO
To you, anyone who keeps his eyes open
is a slanderer. And that little song?
Tell me in confidence: I'm a friend
and won't let it go any further;
was it for you, or for my lady...

SUSANNA *(bewildered, aside)*
Who on earth told him about that?

BASILIO
By the way, my daughter,
it would be wise to warn him:
at table he gazes at her so often
and with such avidity
that if the Count noticed... On that point,
you know, he's ferocious.

SUSANNA
You wretch!
Why do you go around
spreading such lies?

BASILIO
Io! Che ingiustizia! Quel che compro io vendo.
A quel che tutti dicono
io non aggiungo un pelo.

IL CONTE *(sorte dal loco)*
Come, che dicon tutti!

BASILIO
Oh bella!

SUSANNA
Oh cielo!

N°7 *Terzetto*

IL CONTE *(a Basilio)*
Cosa sento! Tosto andate, [13]
e scacciate il seduttor.

BASILIO
In mal punto son qui giunto, [14]
perdonate, oh mio signor.

SUSANNA *(quasi svenuta)*
Che ruina, me meschina,
son oppressa dal dolor.

BASILIO e IL CONTE *(sostenendo Susanna)*
Ah già svien la poverina!
Come, oh Dio, le batte il cor!

BASILIO
Pian pianin su questo seggio.

(Approssimandosi al sedile in atto di farla sedere.)

SUSANNA *(rinviene)*
Dove sono! Cosa veggio!
Che insolenza, andate fuor.

(Si stacca da tutti e due.)

BASILIO
I? You wrong me: I sell only what I buy.
I don't add a jot
to what everyone is saying.

COUNT *(emerging from his hiding-place)*
Really, what is everyone saying?

BASILIO
Very pretty!

SUSANNA
Oh Heaven!

No. 7 Trio

COUNT *(to Basilio)*
What do I hear? Go at once [13]
and send the seducer packing.

BASILIO
My presence is ill-timed. [14]
Pray excuse me, my lord.

SUSANNA *(almost fainting)*
Unhappy me, I'm ruined!
I'm overcome with misery.

BASILIO and COUNT *(supporting Susanna)*
Ah! the poor child's fainted!
Lord, how her heart is beating!

BASILIO
Gently, gently, onto this seat.

(They draw her towards the chair to let her sit down.)

SUSANNA *(reviving)*
Where am I? What's going on?
How dare you! Go away!

(She repulses them both.)

BASILIO *(con malignità)*
Siamo qui per aiutarvi,
è sicuro il vostro onor.

IL CONTE
Siamo qui per aiutarti,
non turbarti, oh mio tesor.

BASILIO *(al Conte)*
Ah, del paggio quel che ho detto
era solo un mio sospetto.

SUSANNA
È un'insidia, una perfidia,
non credete all'impostor.

IL CONTE
Parta, parta il damerino!

SUSANNA e BASILIO
Poverino!

IL CONTE *(ironicamente)*
Poverino!
Ma da me sorpreso ancor.

SUSANNA
Come!

BASILIO
Che!

IL CONTE
Da tua cugina
l'uscio ier trovai rinchiuso;
picchio, m'apre Barbarina,
paurosa fuor dell'uso.
Io, dal muso insospettito,
guardo, cerco in ogni sito,
ed alzando pian pianino
il tappeto al tavolino
vedo il paggio...

BASILIO *(malevolently)*
We're only helping you;
your honour is quite safe.

COUNT
We're only helping you;
do not be alarmed, my dear.

BASILIO *(to the Count)*
What I said about the page
was only my suspicion.

SUSANNA
It's a plot, it's quite untrue;
don't believe this impostor.

COUNT
That young fop must go.

SUSANNA and BASILIO
Poor boy!

COUNT *(ironically)*
Poor boy!
I've found him out again.

SUSANNA
How so? What?

BASILIO
What? How so?

COUNT
Yesterday I found
your cousin's door locked;
I knocked, and Barbarina opened it,
more flustered than usual.
My suspicions aroused by her appearance,
I looked and searched in every corner,
and very, very softly
lifting the tablecloth,
there I saw the page...

(Imita il gesto colla vestaglia, e scopre il paggio.)

(con sopresa)
Ah! cosa veggio!

SUSANNA *(con timore)*
Ah! crude stelle!

BASILIO *(ridendo)*
Ah! meglio ancora!

IL CONTE
Onestissima signora!
Or capisco come va!

SUSANNA
Accader non può di peggio,
giusti Dei! Che mai sarà!

BASILIO
Così fan tutte le belle;
non c'è alcuna novità!

Recitativo

IL CONTE
Basilio, in traccia tosto
di Figaro volate:

(additando Cherubino, che non si muove dal loco)

io vo' ch'ei veda...

SUSANNA *(con vivezza)*
Ed io che senta; andate!

IL CONTE *(a Basilio)*
Restate: *(a Susanna)* che baldanza! E quale scusa
se la colpa è evidente?

SUSANNA
Non ha d'uopo di scusa un'innocente.

(He illustrates his actions with the dress and discovers the page.)

(in surprise)

Ah, what do I see?

SUSANNA *(fearfully)*
Oh, cruel Heavens!

BASILIO *(laughing)*
Better and better!

COUNT
You paragon of virtue!
Now I see how it is.

SUSANNA
Nothing worse could come about.
Heavens above, what's to happen?

BASILIO
Every woman's alike!
There's nothing new about it.

Recitative

COUNT
Basilio, go off
to Figaro at once.

(pointing to Cherubino, who does not move)

I want him to see…

SUSANNA *(animatedly)*
And I want him to hear: go on.

COUNT *(to Basilio)*
Wait! *(to Susanna)* What assurance! What's your excuse
when your guilt is obvious?

SUSANNA
Virtue has no need of excuses.

IL CONTE
Ma costui quando venne?

SUSANNA
Egli era meco
quando voi qui giungeste, e mi chiedea
d'impegnar la padrona
a intercedergli grazia. Il vostro arrivo
in scompiglio lo pose,
ed allor in quel loco si nascose.

IL CONTE
Ma s'io stesso m'assisi
quando in camera entrai!

CHERUBINO *(timidamente)*
Ed allora di dietro io mi celai.

IL CONTE
E quando io là mi posi?

CHERUBINO
Allor io pian mi volsi, e qui m'ascosi.

IL CONTE *(a Susanna)*
Oh ciel, dunque ha sentito
quello ch'io ti dicea!

CHERUBINO
Feci per non sentir quanto potea.

IL CONTE
Ah perfidia!

BASILIO
Frenatevi: vien gente!

IL CONTE *(a Cherubino)*
E voi restate qui, picciol serpente!

(Lo tira giù dal sedile.)

COUNT
But when did he come in?

SUSANNA
He was with me
when you came in here,
and was asking me to beg my lady
to intercede for him: your arrival
threw us into confusion,
and so he hid himself in there.

COUNT
But I sat down there myself
when I came into the room!

CHERUBINO *(timidly)*
Then I hid myself behind it.

COUNT
And when I placed myself there?

CHERUBINO
Then I quietly crept round and hid here.

COUNT *(to Susanna)*
Heavens! Then he heard
all that I was saying to you?

CHERUBINO
I did everything I could not to hear.

COUNT
Deceitful boy!

BASILIO
Restrain yourself: someone's coming.

COUNT *(to Cherubino)*
And you're still there, you little viper!

(He drags him out of the chair.)

Scena VIII

Figaro con bianca veste in mano. Contadini e Contadine vestite di bianco che spargono fiori, raccolti in piccoli panieri, davanti al Conte.

N°8 Coro

CORO
Giovani liete, [15]
fiori spargete
davanti al nobile
nostro signor.
Il suo gran core
vi serba intatto
d'un più bel fiore
l'almo candor.

Recitativo

IL CONTE *(a Figaro con sorpresa)*
Cos'è questa commedia?

FIGARO *(a Susanna, piano)*
Eccoci in danza:
secondami, cor mio.

SUSANNA *(piano a Figaro)*
Non ci ho speranza.

FIGARO *(al Conte)*
Signor, non disdegnate
questo del nostro affetto
meritato tributo: or che aboliste
un diritto sì ingrato a chi ben ama...

IL CONTE
Quel dritto or non v'è più; cosa si brama?

FIGARO
Della vostra saggezza il primo frutto
oggi noi coglierem: le nostre nozze
si son già stabilite. Or a voi tocca

Scene VIII

Enter Figaro with a white veil in his hand; peasants dressed in white scatter flowers arranged in little baskets before the Count.

No. 8 Chorus

CHORUS
Blithe maids, [15]
scatter flowers
before our
noble lord.
His generous heart
has preserved intact for you
the chaste purity
of a still fairer flower.

Recitative

COUNT *(in surprise to Figaro)*
What's all this nonsense?

FIGARO *(softly to Susanna)*
Here we go:
back me up, my dear.

SUSANNA *(softly to Figaro)*
I'm not hopeful.

FIGARO *(to the Count)*
My lord, do not disdain
this humble expression of our affection.
Now that you've abolished
a privilege so painful to lovers…

COUNT
That privilege exists no more: what now?

FIGARO
Today we've come to gather the first fruit
of your generosity: our wedding
is already arranged: may it please you

costei, che un vostro dono
illibata serbò, coprir di questa,
simbolo d'onestà, candida vesta.

IL CONTE *(tra sé)*
Diabolica astuzia!
Ma fingere convien.

(forte)

Son grato, amici,
ad un senso sì onesto!
Ma non merto per questo
né tributi né lodi; e un dritto ingiusto
ne' miei feudi abolendo,
a natura, al dover lor dritti io rendo.

TUTTI
Evviva, evviva, evviva!

SUSANNA *(malignamente)*
Che virtù!

FIGARO
Che giustizia!

IL CONTE *(a Figaro e Susanna)*
A voi prometto
compier la cerimonia:
chiedo sol breve indugio; io voglio in faccia
de' miei più fidi, e con più ricca pompa
rendervi appien felici.

(tra sé)

Marcellina si trovi.

(forte)

Andate, amici.

to crown her, whom this gift of yours
has preserved spotless, with this
white veil, symbol of virtue.

COUNT *(aside)*
Devilish ploy!
But I must dissemble.

(aloud)

My friends, I thank you
for your honest feelings,
but for this I do not deserve
any tribute or praise: It was an unjust privilege,
and by abolishing it in my domain
I have restored to nature and duty their rights.

ALL
Hurrah! hurrah! hurrah!

SUSANNA *(ironically)*
What nobility!

FIGARO
What justice!

COUNT *(to Figaro and Susanna)*
To you I promise
to perform the ceremony,
but give me leave a while.
I wish to complete your happiness
before my closest friends and in richest style.

(aside)

Marcellina must be found.

(aloud)

Leave me, friends.

N°8 Coro

CORO *(spargendo il resto dei fiori)*
Giovani liete,
fiori spargete
davanti al nobile
nostro signor.
Il suo gran core
vi serba intatto
d'un più bel fiore
l'almo candor.

(partono)

Recitativo

FIGARO
Evviva!

SUSANNA
Evviva!

BASILIO
Evviva!

FIGARO *(a Cherubino)*
E voi non applaudite?

SUSANNA
È afflitto, poveretto!
Perché il padron lo scaccia dal castello!

FIGARO
Ah, in un giorno sì bello!

SUSANNA
In un giorno di nozze!

FIGARO
Quando ognuno v'ammira!

CHERUBINO *(s'inginocchia)*
Perdono, mio signor...

No. 8 Chorus

CHORUS *(scattering the remaining flowers)*
Blithe maids,
scatter flowers
before our
noble lord.
His generous heart
has preserved intact for you
the chaste purity
of a still fairer flower.

(exeunt)

Recitative

FIGARO
Hurrah!

SUSANNA
Hurrah!

BASILIO
Hurrah!

FIGARO *(to Cherubino)*
And you're not cheering?

SUSANNA
He's unhappy, poor boy,
because my lord has dismissed him from the palace.

FIGARO
On this happiest of days!

SUSANNA
On a wedding day!

FIGARO
When everyone applauds you!

CHERUBINO *(kneeling)*
Forgive me, my lord...

IL CONTE

Nol meritate.

SUSANNA

Egli è ancora fanciullo!

IL CONTE

Men di quel che tu credi.

CHERUBINO

È ver, mancai; ma dal mio labbro alfine…

IL CONTE *(lo alza)*

Ben ben – io vi perdono.
Anzi farò di più: vacante è un posto
d'uffizial nel reggimento mio;
io scelgo voi; partite tosto – addio.

(Il Conte vuol partire, Susanna e Cherubino l'arrestano)

SUSANNA e FIGARO

Ah, fin domani sol…

IL CONTE

No, parta tosto.

CHERUBINO *(con passione e sospirando)*

A ubbidirvi, signor, son già disposto.

IL CONTE

Via, per l'ultima volta
la Susanna abbracciate.

(Cherubino abbraccia Susanna, che rimane confusa.)

Inaspettato è il colpo.

FIGARO *(a Cherubino)*

Ehi, capitano,
a me pure la mano;

(piano)

COUNT

You don't deserve it.

SUSANNA

He's still a child.

COUNT

Less so than you think.

CHERUBINO

I did wrong, I know; but I'll never mention…

COUNT *(raising him)*

Enough, enough – I pardon you.
Nay, I'll do more: there is a vacancy
for an officer in my regiment;
I nominate you; go at once – goodbye.

(He turns to go; Susanna and Figaro stop him.)

SUSANNA and FIGARO

Ah! just until tomorrow…

COUNT

No, he must go at once.

CHERUBINO *(sighing, with passion)*

I'm ready, my lord, and will obey you.

COUNT

Then embrace Susanna
for the last time.

(Cherubino embraces Susanna, who stands confused.)

That took them by surprise.

FIGARO *(to Cherubino)*

Well, captain,
won't you give me your hand?

(softly)

io vo' parlarti
pria che tu parta.

(con finta gioia)

Addio,
picciolo Cherubino;
come cangia in un punto il tuo destino!

N°9 Aria

FIGARO
Non più andrai, farfallone amoroso, [16]
notte e giorno d'intorno girando;
delle belle turbando il riposo
Narcisetto, Adoncino d'amor.
Non più avrai questi bei pennacchini,
quel cappello leggero e galante,
quella chioma, quell'aria brillante,
quel vermiglio donnesco color.
Tra guerrieri, poffar Bacco!
Gran mustacchi, stretto sacco.
Schioppo in spalla, sciabla al fianco,
collo dritto, muso franco,
un gran casco, o un gran turbante,
molto onor, poco contante!
Ed invece del fandango,
una marcia per il fango.
Per montagne, per valloni, [17]
con le nevi e i solleoni,
al concerto di tromboni,
di bombarde, di cannoni,
che le palle in tutti i tuoni
all'orecchio fan fischiar.
Cherubino alla vittoria:
alla gloria militar.

(Partono tutti al suono d'una marcia.)

Before you go
I want a word with you.

(aloud, with feigned joy)

Goodbye,
master Cherubino!
How your fate changes in a moment!

No. 9 Aria

FIGARO
No more, you amorous butterfly, [16]
will you go fluttering round by night and day,
disturbing the peace of every maid,
you pocket Narcissus, you Adonis of love.
No more will you have those fine feathers,
that light and dashing cap,
those curls, those airs and graces,
that rouged womanish colour.
You'll be among warriors, by Bacchus!
Long moustaches, knapsack tightly on,
musket on your shoulder, sabre at your side,
head erect and bold of visage,
a great helmet or a headdress,
lots of honour, little money,
and instead of the fandango,
marching through the mud.
Over mountains, through valleys, [17]
on snowy days, on dog days,
to the sound of blunderbusses,
shells and cannons,
whose shots make your ears sing
on every note.
Cherubino, on to victory,
on to military glory!

(Exeunt all to the sound of a march.)

ATTO SECONDO

Scena I

Camera ricca con alcova e tre porte.

La Contessa sola: poi Susanna e poi Figaro.

N°10 Cavatina

LA CONTESSA
Porgi, amor, qualche ristoro [18]
al mio duolo, a' miei sospir.
O mi rendi il mio tesoro,
o mi lascia almen morir.

(Susanna entra.)

Scena II

Recitativo

LA CONTESSA
Vieni, cara Susanna,
finiscimi l'istoria!

SUSANNA
È già finita.

LA CONTESSA
Dunque volle sedurti?

SUSANNA
Oh, il signor Conte
non fa tai complimenti
colle donne mie pari;
egli venne a contratto di danari.

LA CONTESSA
Ah, il crudel più non m'ama!

ACT TWO

Scene I

A handsome room with an alcove and three doors.

The Countess, alone; then Susanna and Figaro.

No. 10 Cavatina

COUNTESS
O love, bring some relief [18]
to my sorrow, to my sighs;
O give me back my loved one,
or in mercy let me die.

(Enter Susanna.)

Scene II

Recitative

COUNTESS
Come, dear Susanna,
and tell me the rest of the story.

SUSANNA
There's no more to tell.

COUNTESS
So he tried to make love to you?

SUSANNA
Oh, his lordship
doesn't pay such compliments
to girls like me;
he came to offer me money.

COUNTESS
Cruel man, he loves me no longer!

SUSANNA

E come poi

è geloso di voi?

LA CONTESSA

Come lo sono

i moderni mariti: per sistema
infedeli, per genio capricciosi,
e per orgoglio poi tutti gelosi.
Ma se Figaro t'ama… ei sol potria…

FIGARO *(incomincia a cantare entro le quinte)*

La la la… La la la…

SUSANNA

Eccolo: vieni, amico.
Madama impaziente…

FIGARO *(con ilare disinvoltura)*

A voi non tocca

stare in pena per questo.
Alfin di che si tratta? Al signor Conte
piace la sposa mia,
indi segretamente
ricuperar vorria
il diritto feudale.
Possibile è la cosa, e naturale.

LA CONTESSA

Possibil!

SUSANNA

Natural!

FIGARO

Naturalissima.

E se Susanna vuol, possibilissima.

SUSANNA

Finiscila una volta.

SUSANNA

Yet how

can he be jealous of you?

COUNTESS

That is the way

of modern husbands: on principle
unfaithful, by nature fickle,
and by pride all jealous.
But if Figaro loves you… Only he could…

FIGARO *(singing offstage, then entering)*
La la la… La la la…

SUSANNA
Here he is! Come in, friend:
my lady's getting anxious…

FIGARO *(with cheerful nonchalance)*

You've no cause

to be worried about that.
After all, what's it all about?
My bride attracts his lordship.
And so he'd like
secretly to revive
his feudal right:
it's all possible and natural.

COUNTESS
Possible!

SUSANNA

And natural!

FIGARO

Very natural!

And, if Susanna's willing, perfectly possible.

SUSANNA
Have done with you!

FIGARO

Ho già finito.

Quindi prese il partito
di sceglier me corriero, e la Susanna
consigliera segreta d'ambasciata.
E perch'ella ostinata ognor rifiuta
il diploma d'onor ch'ei le destina,
minaccia di protegger Marcellina.
Questo è tutto l'affare.

SUSANNA

Ed hai coraggio di trattar scherzando
un negozio sì serio?

FIGARO

Non vi basta

che scherzando io ci pensi? Ecco il progetto:

(alla Contessa)

per Basilio un biglietto
io gli fo capitar che l'avvertisca
di certo appuntamento
che per l'ora del ballo
a un amante voi deste...

LA CONTESSA

O ciel! Che sento!

Ad un uom sì geloso!...

FIGARO

Ancora meglio.

Così potrem più presto imbarazzarlo,
confonderlo, imbrogliarlo,
rovesciargli i progetti,
empierlo di sospetti, e porgli in testa
che la moderna festa
ch'ei di fare a me tenta altri a lui faccia;
onde qua perda il tempo, ivi la traccia.
Così quasi *ex abrupto*, e senza ch'abbia

FIGARO

I've done.

That's why he decided
to choose me as courier, and Susanna
as confidential attachée to the embassy;
and because she persistently refuses
the post of honour he had planned for her,
he threatens to favour Marcellina.
That's the whole story.

SUSANNA

And you're so bold as to treat lightly
so serious a matter?

FIGARO

Aren't you glad I can

treat it lightly? Here's my plan.

(to the Countess)

By Basilio I've sent a letter
warning his lordship
about an assignation
which you've made with a lover
for the time of the ball.

COUNTESS

Oh Heaven! what do I hear?

To so jealous a man!...

FIGARO

All the better;

the more easily can we harass him,
confuse him, embroil him,
foil his designs,
fill him with suspicions, and make him
realize that this new game which
he's trying to play on me can be played on him;
so let him waste his time in fruitless search.
Then, without him having made any plan

fatto per frastornarci alcun disegno,
vien l'ora delle nozze, e in faccia a lei

(segnando la Contessa)

non fia, ch'osi d'opporsi ai voti miei.

SUSANNA
È ver, ma in di lui vece
s'opporrà Marcellina.

FIGARO
Aspetta: al Conte
farai subito dir che verso sera
attendati in giardino;
il picciol Cherubino,
per mio consiglio non ancor partito,
da femmina vestito,
faremo che in sua vece ivi sen vada.
Questa è l'unica strada
onde monsù sorpreso da madama
sia costretto a far poi quel che si brama.

LA CONTESSA *(a Susanna)*
Che ti par?

SUSANNA
Non c'è mal.

LA CONTESSA
Nel nostro caso...

SUSANNA
Quand'egli è persuaso... e dove è il tempo?

FIGARO
Ito è il Conte alla caccia, e per qualch'ora
non sarà di ritorno;

(in atto di partire)

to prevent us, the time of our wedding
will suddenly be upon us, and in your presence

(indicating the Countess)

he'd not dare to oppose it.

SUSANNA
That's true, but in his stead
Marcellina will oppose it.

FIGARO
Wait: quickly let the Count know
that towards evening
you'll be waiting in the garden:
we'll get young Cherubino,
whom I advised not to leave just yet,
to go there in your place,
dressed as a woman.
If monsieur is caught by milady,
this is the only way by which
he can be made to grant her wishes.

COUNTESS *(to Susanna)*
What do you think?

SUSANNA
Not bad.

COUNTESS
In our situation...

SUSANNA
When he's determined... Have we time enough?

FIGARO
The Count has gone out hunting,
and won't be back for some hours;

(about to go)

io vado e tosto
Cherubino vi mando; lascio a voi
la cura di vestirlo.

LA CONTESSA
E poi?...

FIGARO
E poi...
Se vuol ballare,
signor Contino,
il chitarrino
le suonerò.

(parte)

Scena III

La Contessa, Susanna, poi Cherubino.

Recitativo

LA CONTESSA
Quanto duolmi, Susanna,
che questo giovinotto abbia del Conte
le stravaganze udite! Ah, tu non sai!...
Ma per qual causa mai
Da me stessa ei non venne?...
Dov'è la canzonetta?

SUSANNA
Eccola: appunto
facciam che ce la canti.
Zitto, vien gente! È desso: avanti, avanti,

(Cherubino entra)

signor uffiziale.

CHERUBINO
Ah, non chiamarmi
con nome sì fatale! Ei mi rammenta

I'll go and send Cherubino
to you at once; I leave to you
the task of disguising him.

COUNTESS

And then?...

FIGARO

And then...

If, my dear Count,
you feel like dancing,
it's I
who'll call the tune.

(exit)

Scene III

The Countess, Susanna, then Cherubino.

Recitative

COUNTESS

I'm grieved, Susanna,
that that youth should have overheard
the Count's follies: you just don't know...
But why ever did he
not come straight to me?...
Where's his song?

SUSANNA

Here it is: and when he comes
let's make him sing it.
Hush, someone's coming: it's he. Come in, come in,

(enter Cherubino)

my gallant captain.

CHERUBINO

Oh don't call me by that
horrid title! It reminds me

che abbandonar degg'io
comare tanto buona...

SUSANNA
E tanto bella!

CHERUBINO *(sospirando)*
Ah sì... certo...

SUSANNA *(imitandolo)*
Ah sì... certo... Ipocritone!
Via presto, la canzone
che stamane a me deste
a madama cantate.

LA CONTESSA
Chi n'è l'autor?

SUSANNA *(additando Cherubino)*
Guardate: egli ha due braccia
di rossor sulla faccia.

LA CONTESSA
Prendi la mia chitarra e l'accompagna.

CHERUBINO
Io sono sì tremante...
ma se madama vuole...

SUSANNA
Lo vuole, sì, lo vuol. Manco parole.

(Susanna fa il ritornello sulla chitarra.)

N°11 Arietta

CHERUBINO
Voi che sapete [19]
che cosa è amor,
donne, vedete
s'io l'ho nel cor.

that I am forced to leave
a godmother so kind.

SUSANNA

And so beautiful!

CHERUBINO *(sighing)*
Ah… yes… indeed!

SUSANNA *(imitating him)*
Ah… yes… indeed… hypocrite!
Make haste, sing to my lady
the song you gave to me
this morning.

COUNTESS
Who wrote it?

SUSANNA *(indicating Cherubino)*
Look: he's blushing
all over his face.

COUNTESS
Take my guitar and accompany him.

CHERUBINO
I'm all atremble…
but if my lady wishes…

SUSANNA
Yes, indeed she does… don't keep her waiting.

(She plays the introduction on the guitar.)

No. 11 Arietta

CHERUBINO
You ladies [19]
who know what love is,
see if it is
what I have in my heart.

Quello ch'io provo
vi ridirò,
è per me nuovo,
capir nol so.
Sento un affetto
pien di desir,
ch'ora è diletto,
ch'ora è martir.
Gelo e poi sento
l'alma avvampar,
e in un momento
torno a gelar.
Ricerco un bene
fuori di me,
non so chi'l tiene,
non so cos'è.
Sospiro e gemo
senza voler,
palpito e tremo
senza saper.
Non trovo pace
notte né dì,
ma pur mi piace
languir così.
Voi che sapete
che cosa è amor,
donne, vedete
s'io l'ho nel cor.

Recitativo

LA CONTESSA
Bravo! Che bella voce! Io non sapea
che cantaste sì bene.

SUSANNA
Oh, in verità
egli fa tutto ben quello ch'ei fa.

All that I feel
I will explain;
since it is new to me,
I don't understand it.
I have a feeling
full of desire,
which now is pleasure,
now is torment.
I freeze, then I feel
my spirit all ablaze,
and the next moment
turn again to ice.
I seek for a treasure
outside of myself;
I know not who holds it
nor what it is.
I sigh and I groan
without wishing to,
I flutter and tremble
without knowing why.
I find no peace
by night or day,
but yet to languish thus
is sheer delight.
You ladies
who know what love is,
see if it is
what I have in my heart.

Recitative

COUNTESS
Bravo! a charming voice!
I didn't know you sang so well.

SUSANNA
Oh, I must say
everything he does, he does well.

Presto a noi, bel soldato.
Figaro v'informò…

CHERUBINO

Tutto mi disse.

SUSANNA

Lasciatemi veder. Andrà benissimo!
Siam d'uguale statura… giù quel manto.

(Gli cava il manto.)

LA CONTESSA

Che fai?

SUSANNA

Niente paura.

LA CONTESSA

E se qualcuno entrasse?

SUSANNA

Entri, che mal facciamo?
La porta chiuderò.

(Chiude la porta.)

Ma come poi
acconciargli i capelli?

LA CONTESSA

Una mia cuffia
prendi nel gabinetto.
Presto!

(Susanna va nel gabinetto a pigliare una cuffia; Cherubino si accosta alla Contessa, e le lascia vedere la patente che terrà in petto; la Contessa la prende, la apre e vede che manca il sigillo.)

Che carta è quella?

CHERUBINO

La patente.

Come along, handsome soldier;
Figaro will have told you...

CHERUBINO

He's told me everything.

SUSANNA

Let me see: this will do splendidly.
We are of equal height... Off with your jacket.

(She takes off his jacket.)

COUNTESS

What are you doing?

SUSANNA

There's nothing to fear.

COUNTESS

But if someone should come in?

SUSANNA

Let him, what harm are we doing?
But I'll lock the door.

(She does so.)

But how am I
to dress his hair?

COUNTESS

Take one of my caps
from my dressing room.
Quickly!

(Susanna goes into the dressing room to get a cap: Cherubino approaches the Countess and shows her his commission in his breast pocket. The Countess takes it, opens it and notices that the seal is missing.)

What is this paper?

CHERUBINO

My commission.

LA CONTESSA
Che sollecita gente!

CHERUBINO
L'ebbi or da Basilio.

LA CONTESSA *(gliela rende)*
Dalla fretta obliato hanno il sigillo.

SUSANNA *(tornando)*
Il sigillo di che?

LA CONTESSA
Della patente.

SUSANNA
Cospetto! Che premura!
Ecco la cuffia.

LA CONTESSA
Spìcciati: va bene!
Miserabili noi se il Conte viene.

N°12 Aria

SUSANNA
Venite, inginocchiatevi; [20]

(prende Cherubino e se lo fa inginocchiare davanti poco discosto dalla Contessa, che siede)

Restate fermo lì.

(lo pettina da un lato; poi lo prende pe 'l mento e lo volge a suo piacere)

Pian piano, or via, giratevi:
Bravo, va ben così.

(Cherubino guarda la Contessa teneramente.)

La faccia ora volgetemi:
Olà, quegli occhi a me.

COUNTESS
They're in a hurry!

CHERUBINO
I've just had it from Basilio.

COUNTESS *(returning it to him)*
In their haste they've forgotten the seal.

SUSANNA *(coming back)*
What seal?

COUNTESS
Of his commission.

SUSANNA
What, so soon!
Here's the cap.

COUNTESS *(to Susanna)*
Hurry! That's right.
Woe betide us if the Count should come.

No. 12 Aria

SUSANNA
Come... kneel down... [20]

(taking Cherubino with her and making him kneel before her, a little way from the Countess, who sits down)

Stay still here...

(combing his hair first from one side. She then takes him by the chin and turns his head about as she wishes)

Keep quiet; now turn round...
Good... that's very good.

(Cherubino looks tenderly towards the Countess.)

Now turn and face me,
here! your eyes towards me...

(seguita ad acconciarlo ed a porgli la cuffia)

Drittissimo: guardatemi.
Madama qui non è.
Più alto quel colletto…
quel ciglio un po' più basso…
le mani sotto il petto…
vedremo poscia il passo
quando sarete in piè.

(piano alla Contessa)

Mirate il bricconcello!
Mirate quanto è bello!
Che furba guardatura!
Che vezzo, che figura!
Se l'amano le femmine [21]
han certo il lor perché.

[1789 version]

N°12a Arietta

SUSANNA
Un moto di gioia [22]
mi sento nel petto,
che annunzia diletto
in mezzo il timor!
Speriam che in contento
finisca l'affanno;
non sempre è tiranno
il fato ed amor.
Di pianti di pene
ognor non si pasce,
talvolta poi nasce
il ben dal dolor:
e quando si crede
più grave il periglio,
brillare si vede
la calma maggior.

(carrying on doing his hair and placing the bonnet on him)

Look straight in front at me...
My lady isn't here.
That collar a bit higher.
Those eyes cast down,
your hands folded before you...
Then let's see how you walk
when you're on your feet.

(softly to the Countess)

Look at the little rascal!
Isn't he handsome?
What roguish glances,
what airs, what graces!
If women fall in love with him, [21]
they have good reason why.

[1789 version]

No. 12a Arietta

SUSANNA
I feel stirrings of joy [22]
in my breast,
which promise pleasure
amid this anxiety.
Let's hope our troubles
will end in happiness;
destiny and love
are not always cruel.
One can't always be feeding
on tears and pain;
sometimes good
comes of sorrow;
and just when you think
the danger is at its height,
you see calmer days
shining ahead.

Recitativo

LA CONTESSA
Quante buffonerie!

SUSANNA
Ma se ne sono
io medesma gelosa…

(prende pe 'l mento Cherubino)

Ehi, serpentello,
volete tralasciar d'esser sì bello!

LA CONTESSA
Finiam le ragazzate: or quelle maniche
oltre il gomito gli alza,
onde più agiatamente
l'abito gli si adatti.

SUSANNA *(eseguisce)*
Ecco.

LA CONTESSA
Più indietro.
Così.

(scoprendo un nastro, onde ha fasciato il braccio)

Che nastro è quello?

SUSANNA
È quel ch'esso involommi.

LA CONTESSA *(stacca il nastro)*
E questo sangue?

CHERUBINO
Quel sangue… io non so come…
poco pria sdrucciolando
in un sasso… la pelle io mi sgraffiai…
e la piaga col nastro io mi fasciai.

Recitative

COUNTESS
This is too silly!

SUSANNA
I'm almost inclined
to be jealous myself.

(taking Cherubino by the chin)

You little scamp,
you've no right to look so pretty!

COUNTESS
No more of this childishness! Now pull these sleeves up
above the elbow,
then the dress will go on
more comfortably.

SUSANNA *(doing so)*
There!

COUNTESS
Still higher,
like that...

(discovering a ribbon tied round his arm)

What's this ribbon?

SUSANNA
That's the one he stole from me.

COUNTESS *(untying the ribbon)*
And this blood?

CHERUBINO
Blood?... I don't know how...
I slipped a little while ago
and grazed myself against a stone...
So I tied up the scratch with this ribbon.

SUSANNA
Mostrate! Non è mal. Cospetto! Ha il braccio
più candido del mio! Qualche ragazza...

LA CONTESSA
E segui a far la pazza?
Va' nel mio gabinetto, e prendi un poco
d'inglese taffetà, ch'è sullo scrigno:

(Susanna parte in fretta.)

In quanto al nastro... inver... per il colore
mi spiacea di privarmene.

SUSANNA *(entra e le dà il taffetà e le forbici)*
Tenete,
e da legargli il braccio?

LA CONTESSA
Un altro nastro
prendi insiem col mio vestito.

CHERUBINO
Ah, più presto m'avria quello guarito!

(Susanna parte per la porta ch'è in fondo e porta seco il mantello di Cherubino.)

LA CONTESSA
Perché? Questo è migliore!

CHERUBINO
Allor che un nastro...
legò la chioma... ovver toccò la pelle...
d'oggetto...

LA CONTESSA
...forestiero,
è buon per le ferite! Non è vero?
Guardate qualità ch'io non sapea!

SUSANNA
Let's see: it's nothing much. Look!
His arm's whiter than mine! Like a girl's…

COUNTESS
Are you still chattering?
Go into my room, and fetch a piece
of plaster which is on my desk.

(Exit Susanna, hurriedly.)

As for this ribbon… I'd say… because of its colour…
I'd like to keep it…

SUSANNA *(re-entering with the plaster and scissors)*
Here you are.
Now what to tie his arm with?

COUNTESS
Bring another ribbon
along with my dress.

CHERUBINO
Ah! that one would have healed me faster.

(exit Susanna by the rear door, taking with her Cherubino's mantle)

COUNTESS
Why? This one is better.

CHERUBINO
But when a ribbon
has bound the hair, or touched the skin
of some…

COUNTESS
…other person,
it's good for wounds, is that it?
That's a virtue I was not aware of!

CHERUBINO
Madama scherza – ed io frattanto parto.

LA CONTESSA
Poverin! Che sventura!

CHERUBINO
Oh, me infelice!

LA CONTESSA
Or piange...

CHERUBINO
Oh ciel! Perché morir non lice!
Forse vicino all'ultimo momento...
questa bocca oseria!

LA CONTESSA
Siate saggio; cos'è questa follia?

(si sente picchiare alla porta)

Chi picchia alla mia porta?

Scena IV

La Contessa, Cherubino e il Conte fuori della porta.

IL CONTE *(fuori della porta)*
Perché chiusa?

LA CONTESSA
Il mio sposo! Oh Dei! Son morta!
Voi qui senza mantello!
In quello stato! Un ricevuto foglio...
la sua gran gelosia!

IL CONTE
Cosa indugiate?

LA CONTESSA
Son sola... anzi son sola...

CHERUBINO
My lady mocks me when I must leave her.

COUNTESS
Poor boy, it's hard!

CHERUBINO
I'm so unhappy!

COUNTESS
What, crying?

CHERUBINO
Oh Heaven! Would that I could die now!
Perhaps near the final moment
these lips would dare…

COUNTESS
Be sensible: what is this nonsense?

(a knock at the door is heard)

Who's knocking at the door?

Scene IV

The Countess, Cherubino, with the Count offstage behind the door.

COUNT *(outside the door)*
Why is this locked?

COUNTESS
My husband! Oh Heavens! I'm lost!
You here without a coat on!
In this state! He'll have had that letter…
and he's so jealous!

COUNT
What is delaying you?

COUNTESS
I'm alone… yes, all alone.

IL CONTE

E a chi parlate?

LA CONTESSA

A voi… certo… a voi stesso…

CHERUBINO

Dopo quel ch'è successo, il suo furore…
non trovo altro consiglio!

(Entra nel gabinetto e chiude.)

LA CONTESSA *(prende la chiave)*

Ah, mi difenda il cielo in tal periglio!

(Corre ad aprire al Conte.)

Scena V

La Contessa ed il Conte da cacciatore.

IL CONTE *(entrando)*

Che novità! Non fu mai vostra usanza
di rinchiudervi in stanza!

LA CONTESSA

È ver; ma io…
io stava qui mettendo…

IL CONTE

Via, mettendo…

LA CONTESSA

… certe robe… era meco la Susanna…
che in sua camera è andata.

IL CONTE

Ad ogni modo
voi non siete tranquilla.
Guardate questo foglio!

COUNT

To whom were you talking?

COUNTESS

To you... of course, to you.

CHERUBINO

After what's happened, he'll be furious...
I don't know what to do!

(Cherubino runs into the dressing room and locks the door.)

COUNTESS *(taking the key)*

Heaven protect me in this danger!

(She hurries to open the door to the Count.)

Scene V

The Countess, and the Count in hunting dress.

COUNT *(entering)*

What does this mean? You never used
to lock yourself in your room!

COUNTESS

I know; but I...

I was in here trying...

COUNT

Go on, trying...

COUNTESS

...some clothes on... Susanna was with me...
but now she's gone to her room.

COUNT

In any case,

you seem perturbed.
Look at this letter.

LA CONTESSA *(tra sé)*

Numi! È il foglio
che Figaro gli scrisse...

(Cherubino fa cadere un tavolino, ed una sedia in gabinetto, con molto strepito.)

IL CONTE

Cos'è questo
strepito? In gabinetto
qualche cosa è caduta.

LA CONTESSA
Io non intesi niente.

IL CONTE
Convien che abbiate i gran pensieri in mente.

LA CONTESSA
Di che?

IL CONTE
Là v'è qualchuno.

LA CONTESSA
Chi volete che sia?

IL CONTE

Io chiedo a voi.
Io vengo in questo punto.

LA CONTESSA
Ah sì, Susanna... appunto...

IL CONTE
Che passò mi diceste alla sua stanza!

LA CONTESSA
Alla sua stanza, o qui – non vidi bene...

IL CONTE
Susanna! E donde viene
che siete sì turbata?

COUNTESS *(aside)*

Heavens! it's the letter

Figaro wrote him!

(Cherubino noisily knocks over a table and chair in the dressing room.)

COUNT

What is that noise?

Something fell
in your room.

COUNTESS
I heard nothing.

COUNT
You must have weighty matters on your mind.

COUNTESS
Of what?

COUNT

There's someone there.

COUNTESS
Who do you think it could be?

COUNT

I'm asking you...

I've only just come in.

COUNTESS
Ah yes, Susanna... of course.

COUNT
But you told me she went to her room.

COUNTESS
To hers or mine, I didn't notice...

COUNT
Then why, if it's Susanna,
are you so agitated?

LA CONTESSA *(con risolino sforzato)*
Per la mia cameriera?

IL CONTE
Io non so nulla;
ma turbata senz'altro.

LA CONTESSA
Ah, questa serva
più che non turba me turba voi stesso.

IL CONTE
È vero, è vero, e lo vedrete adesso.

Scena VI

Susanna entra per la porta ond'è uscita, e si ferma vedendo il Conte, che dalla porta del gabinetto sta favellando.

N°13 Terzetto

IL CONTE
Susanna, or via, sortite, [23]
sortite, io così vo'.

LA CONTESSA *(al Conte, affannata)*
Fermatevi... sentite...
Sortire ella non può.

SUSANNA *(tra sé)*
Cos'è codesta lite!
Il paggio dove andò!

IL CONTE
E chi vietarlo or osa?

LA CONTESSA
Lo vieta l'onestà.
Un abito da sposa
provando ella si sta.

COUNTESS *(with a forced smile)*
About my maid?

COUNT
I don't know;
but certainly you're agitated…

COUNTESS
Rather than agitating me,
which she doesn't, my maid is agitating you.

COUNT
That's true indeed, as you'll see.

Scene VI

Susanna enters by the door through which she went out, but stops on seeing the Count, who is talking by the dressing-room door.

No. 13 Trio

COUNT
Susanna, come out of there, [23]
come out, I command you.

COUNTESS *(distressed, to the Count)*
No, stop… listen…
She can't come out.

SUSANNA *(aside)*
What's this row about?
Where has the page got to?

COUNT
And who dares forbid it?

COUNTESS
Decency forbids it.
She's in there
trying on her wedding dress.

IL CONTE *(tra sé)*
Chiarissima è la cosa:
l'amante qui sarà.

LA CONTESSA *(tra sé)*
Bruttissima è la cosa,
chi sa cosa sarà.

SUSANNA *(tra sé)*
Capisco qualche cosa,
veggiamo come va.

IL CONTE
Dunque parlate almeno.
Susanna, se qui siete...

LA CONTESSA
Nemmen, nemmen, nemmeno,
io v'ordino: tacete.

(Susanna si nasconde entro l'alcova.)

IL CONTE *(tra sé)*
Consorte mia, giudizio,
un scandalo, un disordine,
schiviam per carità!

SUSANNA *(tra sé)*
Oh cielo, un precipizio,
un scandalo, un disordine,
qui certo nascerà.

LA CONTESSA *(tra sé)*
Consorte mio, giudizio,
un scandalo, un disordine,
schiviam per carità!

Recitativo

IL CONTE
Dunque voi non aprite?

COUNT *(aside)*
It's all too plain:
there's a lover in there.

COUNTESS *(aside)*
It's all too horrible:
whatever will happen?

SUSANNA *(aside)*
I think I understand:
let's see how things work out.

COUNT
Well, at least speak,
Susanna, if you're there...

COUNTESS
No, no, you're not to.
I order you, be silent.

(Susanna hides in the alcove.)

COUNT *(aside)*
Be careful, pray!
Try to avoid
an open scandal.

SUSANNA *(aside)*
Oh Heaven! There's bound to be
a catastrophe,
an open scandal.

COUNTESS *(aside)*
Be careful, pray!
Try to avoid
an open scandal.

Recitative

COUNT
Then you won't open it?

LA CONTESSA
E perché deggio
le mie camere aprir?

IL CONTE
Ebben, lasciate,
l'aprirem senza chiavi. Ehi, gente!

LA CONTESSA
Come?
Porreste a repentaglio
d'una dama l'onore?

IL CONTE
È vero, io sbaglio.
Posso senza rumore,
senza scandalo alcun di nostra gente,
andar io stesso a prender l'occorrente.
Attendete pur qui, ma perché in tutto
sia il mio dubbio distrutto anco le porte
io prima chiuderò.

(Chiude a chiave la porta che conduce alle stanze delle cameriere.)

LA CONTESSA *(tra sé)*
Che imprudenza!

IL CONTE
Voi la condiscendenza
di venir meco avrete.

(con affettata ilarità)

Madama, eccovi il braccio, andiamo.

LA CONTESSA
Andiamo.

IL CONTE *(a voce alta, accennando al gabinetto)*
Susanna starà qui finché torniamo.

(partono)

COUNTESS

Why do I have
to open my own room?

COUNT

Very well then; as you please…
We'll open it without the key… Ho there!

COUNTESS

What?
Would you hazard
a lady's reputation?

COUNT

That's true; I was in error.
I can go myself and bring the tools
without any outcry or scandal before the servants.
Kindly remain here…
But so that my suspicions
shall be completely quashed,
first of all I'll lock the other doors.

(He locks the door leading to the servants' quarters.)

COUNTESS *(aside)*

What folly!

COUNT

You will have the goodness
to come with me.

(with affected cheerfulness)

Let me offer you my arm. Let's go.

COUNTESS

Let's go.

COUNT *(indicating the dressing room)*

Susanna will have to stay there till we return.

(exeunt)

Scena VII

Susanna e Cherubino.

N°14 *Duettino*

SUSANNA *(uscendo dall'alcova in fretta; alla porta del gabinetto)*
Aprite, presto, aprite; [24]
aprite, è la Susanna.
Sortite, via sortite,
andate via di qua.

(Cherubino entra confuso e senza fiato.)

CHERUBINO
Oimè, che scena orribile!
Che gran fatalità!

(Si accostano or ad una, or ad un'altra porta, e le trovano tutte chiuse.)

SUSANNA
Di qua, di qua, di là.

SUSANNA e CHERUBINO
Le porte son serrate,
che mai, che mai sarà!

CHERUBINO
Qui perdersi non giova.

SUSANNA
V'uccide se vi trova.

CHERUBINO *(affacciandosi alla finestra)*
Veggiamo un po' qui fuori.
Dà proprio nel giardino.

(facendo moto di saltar giù)

SUSANNA *(trattenendolo)*
Fermate, Cherubino!
Fermate per pietà!

Scene VII

Susanna and Cherubino.

No. 14 Duet

SUSANNA *(rushing out of the alcove; by the dressing-room door)*
Open quickly, open; [24]
open, it's Susanna.
Come out of there…
You must get away at once.

(Cherubino comes in, breathless and confused.)

CHERUBINO
Oh dear, what a terrible scene!
What a dreadful thing to happen!

(They try first one door, then another, but find them all locked.)

SUSANNA
This way, this way, that way!

SUSANNA and CHERUBINO
The doors are locked.
Whatever shall we do?

CHERUBINO
We can't give up.

SUSANNA
He'll kill you if he finds you.

CHERUBINO *(looking out of the window)*
Just let me look outside here.
It gives on to the garden.

(He is about to jump out.)

SUSANNA *(stopping him)*
Stop, Cherubino!
Don't, for pity's sake!

CHERUBINO
Qui perdersi non giova:
m'uccide se mi trova.

SUSANNA *(trattenendolo sempre)*
Tropp'alto per un salto.
Fermate per pietà!

CHERUBINO *(si scioglie)*
Lasciami, pria di nuocerle
nel foco volerei.
Abbraccio te per lei -
addio, così si fa.

SUSANNA
Ei va a perire, oh Dei!
Fermate per pietà; fermate!

(Cherubino salta fuori; Susanna mette un alto grido, siede un momento, poi va alla finestra.)

Recitativo

SUSANNA
Oh, guarda il demonietto! Come fugge!
È già un miglio lontano.
Ma non perdiamci invano.
Entriam nel gabinetto,
venga poi lo smargiasso, io qui l'aspetto.

(Entra nel gabinetto e si chiude dietro la porta.)

Scena VIII

La Contessa, il Conte con martello e tenaglia in mano; al suo arrivo esamina tutte le porte.

IL CONTE
Tutto è come il lasciai: volete dunque
aprir voi stessa, o deggio…

(in atto di aprir a forza la porta)

CHERUBINO
We can't give up:
he'll kill me if he finds me.

SUSANNA *(still holding him back)*
It's too high to jump.
Don't, for pity's sake!

CHERUBINO *(freeing himself)*
Let me go: rather than harm her
I'd leap into the fire.
I embrace her through you.
Farewell; so be it!

SUSANNA
He'll kill himself, for certain.
Stop, for pity's sake!

(Cherubino jumps out; Susanna lets out a shriek, sits down for a moment, then goes to the window.)

Recitative

SUSANNA
Just look at the little demon! How he runs!
He's a mile away already.
There's no time to lose, though.
I'll go into the dressing room;
let the blusterer come: I'm ready for him.

(Susanna goes into the dressing room and locks the door behind her.)

Scene VIII

The Countess and the Count with tools for opening the door; he examines all the doors.

COUNT
All is as I left it; so will you
open it yourself, or must I…

(about to force the door open)

LA CONTESSA

Ahimé, fermate,
e ascoltatemi un poco.

(Il Conte getta il martello e la tenaglia sopra una sedia.)

Mi credete capace
di mancar al dover?

IL CONTE

Come vi piace.
Entro quel gabinetto
chi v'è chiuso vedrò.

LA CONTESSA *(timida e tremante)*

Sì, lo vedrete...
Ma uditemi tranquillo.

IL CONTE

Non è dunque Susanna!

LA CONTESSA

No, ma invece è un oggetto
che ragion di sospetto
non vi deve lasciar. Per questa sera...
una burla innocente...
di far si disponeva... ed io vi giuro...
che l'onor... l'onestà...

IL CONTE

Chi è dunque! Dite...
l'ucciderò.

LA CONTESSA

Sentite!
Ah, non ho cor!

IL CONTE

Parlate.

LA CONTESSA

È un fanciullo...

COUNTESS

Alas! Stay

and hear me for a moment.

(The Count throws the hammer and pliers on a chair.)

Do you think me capable
of failing in my duty?

COUNT

As you please.

I'm going into that room
to see who's locked in there.

COUNTESS *(in fear and trembling)*

Yes, you'll see…

But listen to me calmly.

COUNT

So it's not Susanna!

COUNTESS

No, but it's someone else
whom you could not reasonably
allow yourself to suspect: for tonight
I was preparing a harmless
diversion… and I swear to you
that my honour… my honesty…

COUNT

Who is it? Tell me…

I'll kill him.

COUNTESS

Listen.

Oh, I dare not.

COUNT

Speak out.

COUNTESS

He's a child…

IL CONTE
Un fanciul!...

LA CONTESSA
Sì... Cherubino...

IL CONTE *(tra sé)*
E mi farà il destino
ritrovar questo paggio in ogni loco!

(alla Contessa)

Come? Non è partito? Scellerati!
Ecco i dubbi spiegati, ecco l'imbroglio,
ecco il raggiro onde m'avverte il foglio.

N°15 Finale

IL CONTE *(alla porta del gabinetto, con impeto)*
Esci omai, garzon malnato, [25]
sciagurato, non tardar.

LA CONTESSA *(ritira a forza il Conte)*
Ah, signore, quel furore
per lui fammi il cor tremar.

IL CONTE
E d'opporvi ancor osate?

LA CONTESSA
No, sentite...

IL CONTE
Via, parlate.

LA CONTESSA
Giuro al ciel ch'ogni sospetto...
e lo stato in che il trovate...
sciolto il collo... nudo il petto...

IL CONTE
Sciolto il collo... Nudo il petto... Seguitate!

COUNT

A child?…

COUNTESS

Yes, Cherubino.

COUNT *(aside)*

Has destiny decreed that I'm to find
that page wherever I go?

(to the Countess)

What! Hasn't he gone? The scoundrels!
This explains my doubts, the confusion,
the plot of which the letter warned me.

No. 15 Finale

COUNT *(vehemently, at the dressing-room door)*

Now out you come, you imp of Satan, [25]
you villain, without delay.

COUNTESS *(restraining the Count by force)*

Oh my lord, your anger
makes my heart tremble for him.

COUNT

You still dare to cross me?

COUNTESS

No, listen…

COUNT

Go on, speak.

COUNTESS

I swear to Heaven that your suspicions…
The state in which you'll find him…
His collar untied… his chest bare…

COUNT

His collar untied?… His chest bare?… Pray continue…

LA CONTESSA
Per vestir femminee spoglie…

IL CONTE
Ah comprendo, indegna moglie,
mi vo' tosto vendicar.

LA CONTESSA
Mi fa torto quel trasporto,
m'oltraggiate a dubitar.

IL CONTE
Qua la chiave!

LA CONTESSA
Egli è innocente.

(dandogli la chiave)

Voi sapete…

IL CONTE
Non so niente.
Va' lontan dagli occhi miei,
un'infida, un'empia sei
e mi cerchi d'infamar.

LA CONTESSA
Vado… sì… ma…

IL CONTE
Non ascolto.

LA CONTESSA
Non son rea.

IL CONTE
Vel leggo in volto!
Mora, mora, e più non sia [26]
ria cagion del mio penar.

LA CONTESSA
Ah, la cieca gelosia
qualche eccesso gli fa far.

COUNTESS
So as to dress him up as a woman…

COUNT
Ah, I see; you shameless creature,
I'll punish him for this.

COUNTESS
Your anger does me wrong,
your suspicion is an insult.

COUNT
Give me the key!

COUNTESS
He is innocent,

(handing him the key)

And you know it…

COUNT
I know nothing of the sort.
Hence from my sight!
You are faithless, wanton…
You've sought to disgrace me.

COUNTESS
I'll go… yes… but…

COUNT
I'll not hear you.

COUNTESS
I am guiltless.

COUNT
I can read it in your face.
He shall die, die and I'll be rid [26]
of the source of all my torment!

COUNTESS
Oh, to what extreme will
his blind fury lead him?

Scena IX

I suddetti e Susanna.

(Il Conte apre il gabinetto e Susanna esce sulla porta, ed ivi si ferma.)

IL CONTE e LA CONTESSA
Susanna!

SUSANNA
Signore, [27]
cos'è quel stupore?
Il brando prendete,
il paggio uccidete,
quel paggio malnato,
vedetelo qua.

IL CONTE *(tra sé)*
Che scola! La testa
girando mi va.

LA CONTESSA *(tra sé)*
Che storia è mai questa,
Susanna v'è là.

SUSANNA *(tra sé)*
Confusa han la testa,
non san come va.

IL CONTE
Sei sola?

SUSANNA
Guardate,
qui ascoso sarà.

IL CONTE
Guardiamo, guardiamo
qui ascoso sarà.

(Entra nel gabinetto.)

Scene IX

The Countess, the Count and Susanna.

(The Count opens the dressing room door and Susanna steps out, staying in the doorway.)

COUNT and COUNTESS
Susanna!

SUSANNA
My lord! [27]
Why this astonishment?
You've drawn your sword
to kill the page –
well, here you see
that imp of Satan.

COUNT *(aside)*
What confusion!
My head is spinning.

COUNTESS *(aside)*
What can have happened?
Susanna in there?

SUSANNA *(aside)*
They're both baffled
and can't understand.

COUNT *(to Susanna)*
Are you alone?

SUSANNA
Look and see
who can be hidden there.

COUNT
Let's see, let's see,
who is hidden in there.

(He goes into the dressing room.)

LA CONTESSA
Susanna, son morta,
il fiato mi manca.

SUSANNA *(addita alla Contessa la finestra onde è saltato Cherubino)*
Più lieta, più franca,
in salvo è di già.

IL CONTE *(esce dal gabinetto)*
Che sbaglio mai presi!
Appena lo credo;
se a torto v'offesi
perdono vi chiedo;
ma far burla simile
è poi crudeltà.

LA CONTESSA e SUSANNA
Le vostre follie
non mertan pietà.

IL CONTE
Io v'amo.

LA CONTESSA
Nol dite!

IL CONTE
Vel giuro.

LA CONTESSA
Mentite.
Son l'empia, l'infida
che ognora v'inganna.

IL CONTE
Quell'ira, Susanna,
m'aita a calmar.

SUSANNA
Così si condanna
chi può sospettar.

COUNTESS
Susanna, I'm fainting;
I can't breathe.

SUSANNA *(showing the Countess the window from which Cherubino jumped)*
Don't worry, take heart now,
he's already in safety.

COUNT *(coming out in confusion)*
How could I make such a mistake!
I can hardly believe it.
If I did you wrong,
I beg your forgiveness;
but to play such a jest
is sheer cruelty.

SUSANNA and COUNTESS
Your wild accusations
do not deserve to be pardoned.

COUNT
I love you!

COUNTESS
Do not say that!

COUNT
I swear it!

COUNTESS
That is untrue!
I'm a faithless, wanton creature
who's always deceiving you.

COUNT
Help me, Susanna,
to calm her anger.

SUSANNA
This is the punishment
for your suspicions.

LA CONTESSA
Adunque la fede
d'un'anima amante
sì fiera mercede
doveva sperar?

SUSANNA *(in atto di preghiera)*
Signora!

IL CONTE *(in atto di preghiera)*
Rosina!

LA CONTESSA *(al Conte)*
Crudele!
Più quella non sono;
ma il misero oggetto
del vostro abbandono,
che avete diletto
di far disperar.

IL CONTE
Confuso, pentito,
son troppo punito,
abbiate pietà.

SUSANNA
Confuso, pentito,
è troppo punito,
abbiate pietà.

LA CONTESSA
Soffrir sì gran torto
quest'alma non sa.

IL CONTE
Ma il paggio rinchiuso?...

LA CONTESSA
Fu sol per provarvi.

IL CONTE
Ma i tremiti, i palpiti?...

COUNTESS
So this is the reward
I can expect
for the loyalty
of my faithful heart!

SUSANNA *(pleading)*
My lady!

COUNT *(pleading)*
Rosina!

COUNTESS *(to the Count)*
Cruel man!
I am no longer she,
but the wretched object
of your neglect,
whom you delight
to make suffer.

COUNT
Confused and repentant,
I'm sufficiently punished;
have pity now.

SUSANNA
Confused and repentant,
he's sufficiently punished;
have pity now.

COUNTESS
My heart cannot bear
so great a wrong.

COUNT
But the page locked in there?...

COUNTESS
It was only to test you.

COUNT
And all your trembling?...

LA CONTESSA
Fu sol per burlarvi.

IL CONTE
Ma un foglio sì barbaro?

LA CONTESSA e SUSANNA
Di Figaro è il foglio,
e a voi per Basilio.

IL CONTE
Ah perfidi! Io voglio…

LA CONTESSA e SUSANNA
Perdono non merta
chi agli altri nol da.

IL CONTE
Ebben, se vi piace
comune è la pace;
Rosina inflessibile
con me non sarà.

LA CONTESSA
Ah quanto, Susanna,
son dolce di core!
Di donne al furore
chi più crederà?

SUSANNA
Cogli uomin, signora,
girate, volgete,
vedrete che ognora
si cade poi là.

IL CONTE
Guardatemi…

LA CONTESSA
Ingrato!

COUNTESS
Only to tease you.

COUNT
But this cruel letter?

COUNTESS and SUSANNA
Figaro wrote it,
and sent it by Basilio...

COUNT
The traitors! I'll...

COUNTESS and SUSANNA
He who can't forgive others
doesn't deserve to be forgiven.

COUNT
Well then, if you will,
let's make peace all round;
Rosina, do not be
so harsh to me.

COUNTESS
Oh Susanna,
how soft-hearted I am!
Who would ever believe
in a woman's fury?

SUSANNA
With men, my lady,
you turn and turn about,
but you see it always
ends like this.

COUNT
Look at me...

COUNTESS
Ungrateful!

IL CONTE
Ho torto, e mi pento.

(Bacia e ribacia la mano della Contessa.)

IL CONTE
Da questo momento
quest'alma a conoscervi
apprender potrà.

LA CONTESSA
Da questo momento
quest'alma a conoscermi
apprender potrà.

SUSANNA
Da questo momento
quest'alma a conoscerla
apprender potrà.

Scena X

I suddetti e Figaro.

FIGARO *(entrando)*
Signori, di fuori [28]
son già i suonatori.
Le trombe sentite,
i pifferi udite,
tra canti, tra balli
de' nostri vassalli
corriamo, voliamo
le nozze a compir.

(prendendo Susanna sotto il braccio)

IL CONTE
Pian piano, men fretta;

FIGARO
La turba m'aspetta.

COUNT
I wronged you, and I repent it!

(He kisses the Countess's hand repeatedly.)

COUNT
From this moment
my heart will learn
to know you better.

COUNTESS
From this moment
his heart will learn
to know me better.

SUSANNA
From this moment
his heart will learn
to know her better.

Scene X

The above and Figaro.

FIGARO *(entering)*
My lord and lady, [28]
the musicians are outside:
you can hear
the trumpeters and the pipers.
With the singing and dancing
of your vassals,
let us hasten
to celebrate our wedding!

(taking Susanna by the arm)

COUNT
One moment: not so fast.

FIGARO
The crowd is waiting.

IL CONTE
Un dubbio toglietemi
in pria di partir.

LA CONTESSA, SUSANNA e FIGARO *(piano)*
La cosa è scabrosa;
com'ha da finir!

IL CONTE *(piano)*
Con arte le carte
convien qui scoprir.

(mostrandogli il foglio ricevuto da Basilio)

Conoscete, signor Figaro, [29]
questo foglio chi vergò?

FIGARO *(finge d'esaminarlo)*
Nol conosco…

SUSANNA *(a Figaro)*
Nol conosci?

FIGARO
No.

CONTESSA *(a Figaro)*
Nol conosci?

FIGARO
No.

COUNT *(a Figaro)*
Nol conosci?

FIGARO
No.

SUSANNA, LA CONTESSA e IL CONTE *(a Figaro)*
Nol conosci?

FIGARO
No, no, no!

COUNT
Before you go,
remove a doubt of mine.

COUNTESS, SUSANNA and FIGARO *(softly)*
This is getting difficult;
how will it end?

COUNT *(softly)*
Now I must
play my cards carefully.

(showing the letter received from Basilio)

Master Figaro, do you know [29]
who penned this letter?

FIGARO *(pretending to examine it)*
I've no idea.

SUSANNA *(to Figaro)*
You've no idea?

FIGARO
No.

COUNTESS *(to Figaro)*
You've no idea?

FIGARO
No.

COUNT *(to Figaro)*
You've no idea?

FIGARO
No.

SUSANNA, COUNTESS and COUNT *(to Figaro)*
You've no idea?

FIGARO
No, no, no!

SUSANNA
E nol desti a Don Basilio?

LA CONTESSA
Per recarlo?

IL CONTE
Tu c'intendi.

FIGARO
Oibò, oibò.

SUSANNA
E non sai del damerino…

LA CONTESSA
Che stasera nel giardino…

IL CONTE
Già capisci…

FIGARO
Io non lo so.

IL CONTE
Cerchi invan difesa e scusa.
Il tuo ceffo già t'accusa,
vedo ben che vuoi mentir.

FIGARO *(al Conte)*
Mente il ceffo, io già non mento.

LA CONTESSA e SUSANNA *(a Figaro)*
Il talento aguzzi invano
palesato abbiam l'arcano,
non v'è nulla da ridir.

IL CONTE
Che rispondi?

FIGARO
Niente, niente.

SUSANNA
Didn't you give it to Don Basilio?

COUNTESS
To deliver?

COUNT
You're deceiving me.

FIGARO
Oh my, oh my.

SUSANNA
And you don't know about the gallant…

COUNTESS
This evening in the garden…

COUNT
You know now…

FIGARO
I've no idea.

COUNT
In vain you seek a defence or an excuse.
Your very face accuses you;
I can see you're trying to lie.

FIGARO *(to the Count)*
My face is the liar, not I!

COUNTESS and SUSANNA *(to Figaro)*
You sharpen your wits in vain;
we've revealed the secret,
there's no more to be said.

COUNT
What's your answer?

FIGARO
Nothing, nothing.

IL CONTE
Dunque accordi?

FIGARO
Non accordo.

SUSANNA e LA CONTESSA *(a Figaro)*
Eh via, chètati, balordo,
la burletta ha da finir.

FIGARO *(prende Susanna sotto il braccio)*
Per finirla lietamente
e all'usanza teatrale
un'azion matrimoniale
le faremo ora seguir.

SUSANNA e FIGARO *(al Conte)*
Deh signor, nol contrastate,
consolate i miei desir.

LA CONTESSA *(al Conte)*
Deh signor, nol contrastate,
consolate i lor desir.

IL CONTE *(tra sé)*
Marcellina, Marcellina!
Quanto tardi a comparir!

Scena XI

Entra Antonio giardiniere, mezzo ubriaco, con un vaso di garofani schiacciato.

ANTONIO
Ah, signore… signor…

IL CONTE
Cosa è stato?…

ANTONIO
Che insolenza! Chi 'l fece! Chi fu?

COUNT
So you admit it?

FIGARO
No, I don't, sir.

SUSANNA and COUNTESS *(to Figaro)*
Hold your tongue, stupid,
this comedy must be ended.

FIGARO *(taking Susanna by the arm)*
Then to end it happily
according to theatrical practice,
let a marriage ceremony
now follow.

SUSANNA and FIGARO *(to the Count)*
Oh my lord, do not refuse;
grant my wishes.

COUNTESS *(to the Count)*
Oh my lord, do not refuse;
grant their wishes.

COUNT *(aside)*
Marcellina, Marcellina,
how slow you are in coming!

Scene XI

Enter Antonio the gardener, half drunk, with a broken pot of carnations.

ANTONIO
Oh my lord... my lord...

COUNT
What's the matter?...

ANTONIO
How dare he! Who did it? What was it?

LA CONTESSA, SUSANNA, IL CONTE e FIGARO
Cosa dici, cos'hai, cosa è nato?

ANTONIO
Ascoltate...

LA CONTESSA, SUSANNA, IL CONTE e FIGARO
Via, parla, di', su.

ANTONIO
Dal balcone che guarda in giardino
mille cose ogni dì gittar veggio,
e poc'anzi, può darsi di peggio,
vidi un uom, signor mio, gittar giù.

IL CONTE
Dal balcone?

ANTONIO *(mostrandogli il vaso di fiori schiacciato)*
Vedete i garofani?

IL CONTE
In giardino?

ANTONIO
Sì!

SUSANNA e LA CONTESSA *(piano a Figaro)*
Figaro, all'erta.

IL CONTE
Cosa sento!

SUSANNA, LA CONTESSA e FIGARO *(piano)*
Costui ci sconcerta. *(forte)*
Quel briaco che viene far qui?

IL CONTE *(ad Antonio)*
Dunque un uom... ma dov'è, dov'è gito?

ANTONIO
Ratto, ratto, il birbone è fuggito
e ad un tratto di vista m'uscì.

COUNTESS, SUSANNA, COUNT and FIGARO
What's he saying? What's wrong? What's happened?

ANTONIO
Listen...

COUNTESS, SUSANNA, COUNT and FIGARO
Go on, then, speak.

ANTONIO
Every day I see all kinds of things thrown
from the balcony overlooking the garden;
but just now (it couldn't be worse)
I saw a man, my lord, thrown down!

COUNT
From the balcony?

ANTONIO *(showing them the broken flower pot)*
D'you see these carnations?

COUNT
Into the garden?

ANTONIO
Yes!

SUSANNA and COUNTESS *(softly to Figaro)*
Figaro, think quickly!

COUNT
What do I hear?

SUSANNA, COUNTESS and FIGARO *(softly)*
He's taken aback. *(loudly)*
What's this drunkard doing in here?

COUNT *(to Antonio)*
So you saw a man: where did he get to?

ANTONIO
The scoundrel took to his heels
and was out of sight at once.

SUSANNA *(piano a Figaro)*
Sai che il paggio…

FIGARO *(piano a Susanna)*
So tutto, lo vidi.
Ah, ah, ah!

IL CONTE *(a Figaro)*
Taci là.

ANTONIO *(a Figaro)*
Cosa ridi?

FIGARO *(ad Antonio)*
Tu sei cotto dal sorger del dì.

IL CONTE *(ad Antonio)*
Or ripetimi: un uom dal balcone?…

ANTONIO
Dal balcone…

IL CONTE
In giardino?…

ANTONIO
In giardino.

SUSANNA, LA CONTESSA e FIGARO
Ma, signore, se in lui parla il vino!

IL CONTE *(ad Antonio)*
Segui pure, né in volto il vedesti?

ANTONIO
No, nol vidi.

SUSANNA e LA CONTESSA *(piano a Figaro)*
Olá, Figaro, ascolta!

FIGARO *(ad Antonio)*
Via, piangione, sta' zitto una volta,
per tre soldi far tanto tumulto!

SUSANNA *(softly to Figaro)*
You must know it was the page…

FIGARO *(softly to Susanna)*
I know, I saw him.

Ha, ha, ha!

COUNT *(to Figaro)*
Be quiet,sir.

ANTONIO *(to Figaro)*
What's there to laugh at?

FIGARO *(to Antonio)*
You're drunk from morn till night.

COUNT *(to Antonio)*
Now tell me again, a man from the balcony?…

ANTONIO
From the balcony…

COUNT
Into the garden?…

ANTONIO
Into the garden.

SUSANNA, COUNTESS and FIGARO
My lord, it's the wine in him talking!

COUNT *(to Antonio)*
Go on though: didn't you see his face?

ANTONIO
No, I didn't.

SUSANNA and COUNTESS *(softly to Figaro)*
Figaro, did you hear that?

FIGARO *(to Antonio)*
You whining old fool, do be quiet,
making such a fuss over nothing!

Giacché il fatto non può star occulto,
sono io stesso saltato di lì.

IL CONTE and ANTONIO
Chi? Voi stesso?

SUSANNA e LA CONTESSA *(piano)*
Che testa! Che ingegno!

FIGARO *(al Conte)*
Che stupor!

IL CONTE
Già creder nol posso.

ANTONIO *(a Figaro)*
Come mai diventaste sì grosso?
Dopo il salto non foste così.

FIGARO
A chi salta succede così.

ANTONIO
Ch'il direbbe?

SUSANNA e LA CONTESSA *(piano)*
Ed insiste quel pazzo!

IL CONTE *(ad Antonio)*
Tu che dici?

ANTONIO
A me parve il ragazzo.

IL CONTE
Cherubin!

SUSANNA e LA CONTESSA *(piano)*
Maledetto!

Since the fact can't be concealed,
it was I who jumped down from there.

COUNT and ANTONIO
What? It was you?

SUSANNA and COUNTESS *(softly)*
What presence of mind!

FIGARO *(to the Count)*
Why so surprised?

COUNT
I just can't believe it.

ANTONIO *(to Figaro)*
How have you grown so tall, then?
After the jump you weren't so big.

FIGARO
Jumping does that to one.

ANTONIO
Who'd have thought it?

SUSANNA and COUNTESS *(softly)*
The fool is persistent!

COUNT *(to Antonio)*
You, what do you say?

ANTONIO
It looked like that boy to me.

COUNT
Cherubino!

SUSANNA and COUNTESS *(softly)*
Wretched man!

FIGARO
Esso appunto
da Siviglia a cavallo qui giunto,
da Siviglia ov'ei forse sarà.

ANTONIO
Questo no, questo no, che il cavallo
io non vidi saltare di là.

IL CONTE
Che pazienza! Finiam questo ballo!

SUSANNA e LA CONTESSA *(piano)*
Come mai, giusto ciel, finirà?

IL CONTE *(a Figaro)*
Dunque tu..

FIGARO
Saltai giù.

IL CONTE
Ma perché?

FIGARO
Il timor…

IL CONTE
Che timor?

FIGARO *(additando la camera delle serve)*
Là rinchiuso,
aspettando quel caro visetto…
Tippe tappe, un sussurro fuor d'uso…
voi gridaste… lo scritto biglietto…
saltai giù dal terrore confuso…
e stravolto m'ho un nervo del piè!

(fingendo d'aversi stroppiato il piede) [30]

ANTONIO *(porgendo a Figaro alcune carte chiuse)*
Vostre dunque saran queste carte
che perdeste?

FIGARO

Of course, it was him,
back on horseback from Seville,
from Seville where he'd been.

ANTONIO
No, no, that's not so.
I didn't see any horse jump down.

COUNT
Give me patience! Let's have done with this nonsense.

SUSANNA and COUNTESS *(softly)*
Merciful Heaven, how will this end?

COUNT *(to Figaro)*
So it was you...

FIGARO

I jumped down.

COUNT

And why?

FIGARO
I was afraid...

COUNT

Afraid of what?

FIGARO *(indicating the servants' quarters)*

I was shut up in there
waiting for that dear little face...
There was an unusual coming and going
and noise... you were shouting, there was
that letter... I lost my nerve and jumped
down in terror and wrenched a muscle in my foot!

(rubbing his foot as if he had hurt it) [30]

ANTONIO *(handing some folded papers to Figaro)*
Then these letters which you dropped
will be yours?

IL CONTE *(togliendogliele)*
Olà, porgile a me.

FIGARO *(piano alla Contessa e Susanna)*
Sono in trappola.

SUSANNA e LA CONTESSA *(piano a Figaro)*
Figaro, all'erta.

IL CONTE *(apre il foglio e lo chiude tosto)*
Dite un po', questo foglio cos'è?

FIGARO *(cavando di tasca alcune carte per guardare)*
Tosto, tosto... ne ho tanti – aspettate.

ANTONIO
Sarà forse il sommario de' debiti.

FIGARO
No, la lista degli osti.

IL CONTE *(a Figaro)*
Parlate.

(ad Antonio)

E tu lascialo.

SUSANNA e LA CONTESSA *(ad Antonio)*
Lascialo, e parti.

FIGARO *(ad Antonio)*
Lasciami, e parti.

ANTONIO
Parto, sì, ma se torno a trovarti...

(parte)

FIGARO
Vanne, vanne, non temo di te.

IL CONTE *(riapre la carta e poi tosto la chiude; a Figaro)*
Dunque?...

COUNT *(seizing them)*
Here, give them to me.

FIGARO *(softly to Susanna and the Countess)*
I'm caught in a trap.

SUSANNA and COUNTESS *(softly to Figaro)*
Figaro, think quickly!

COUNT *(opening the paper, then promptly refolding it)*
Well, tell me, what's this paper?

FIGARO *(taking some letters from his pocket and looking at them)*
Wait just a moment... I've so many.

ANTONIO
I expect it'll be a list of his debts.

FIGARO
No, a list of the tavern-keepers.

COUNT *(to Figaro)*
Speak up.

(to Antonio)

And you, let him be.

SUSANNA and COUNTESS *(to Antonio)*
Let him be and go away!

FIGARO *(to Antonio)*
Let me be and go away!

ANTONIO
All right, I'll go, but if I catch you again!...

(exit)

FIGARO
Oh go away: I'm not afraid of you.

COUNT *(opening the letter again and refolding it; to Figaro)*
Well?...

LA CONTESSA *(piano a Susanna)*
O ciel! La patente del paggio!

SUSANNA *(piano a Figaro)*
Giusti Dei, la patente!

IL CONTE *(a Figaro, ironicamente)*
Coraggio!

FIGARO *(come in atto di risovvenirsi della cosa)*
Uh, che testa! Questa è la patente
che poc'anzi il fanciullo mi diè.

IL CONTE
Per che fare?

FIGARO *(imbrogliato)*
Vi manca...

IL CONTE
Vi manca?

LA CONTESSA *(piano a Susanna)*
Il suggello.

SUSANNA *(piano a Figaro)*
Il suggello.

IL CONTE *(a Figaro, che finge di pensare)*
Rispondi!

FIGARO
È l'usanza...

IL CONTE
Su via, ti confondi?

FIGARO
È l'usanza di porvi il suggello.

COUNTESS *(softly to Susanna)*
Oh Heavens! the page's commission!

SUSANNA *(softly to Figaro)*
Good Lord! the commission!

COUNT *(ironically to Figaro)*
Take courage!

FIGARO *(as if recollecting something)*
Oh what a head! It's the commission
the boy gave me a while ago.

COUNT
What for?

FIGARO *(embarrassed)*
It lacked...

COUNT
It lacked?

COUNTESS *(softly to Susanna)*
The seal!

SUSANNA *(softly to Figaro)*
The seal!

COUNT *(to Figaro, who pretends to be thinking)*
Well, answer!

FIGARO
It's usually...

COUNT
Go on, why hesitate?

FIGARO
It is usually sealed.

IL CONTE *(guarda e vede che manca il sigillo; guasta il foglio e con somma collera lo getta)*
Questo birbo mi toglie il cervello,
tutto, tutto è un mistero per me.

SUSANNA e LA CONTESSA *(piano)*
Se mi salvo da questa tempesta
più non avvi naufragio per me.

FIGARO *(piano)*
Sbuffa invano e la terra calpesta;
poverino, ne sa men di me.

Scena XII

I suddetti, Marcellina, Bartolo e Basilio

MARCELLINA, BASILIO e BARTOLO *(entrando, al Conte)*
Voi signor, che giusto siete [31]
ci dovete or ascoltar.

IL CONTE *(tra sé)*
Son venuti a vendicarmi.
Io mi sento consolar.

SUSANNA, LA CONTESSA e FIGARO *(piano)*
Son venuti a sconcertarmi.
Qual rimedio ritrovar?

FIGARO *(al Conte)*
Son tre stolidi, tre pazzi,
cosa mai vengono a far?

IL CONTE
Pian pianin, senza schiamazzi
dica ognun quel che gli par.

MARCELLINA
Un impegno nuziale
ha costui con me contratto.
E pretendo che il contratto
deva meco effettuar.

COUNT *(seeing the paper lacks the seal, he crumples it up and throws it aside in a fury)*
This rascal's driving me mad.
The whole thing's a mystery to me.

SUSANNA and COUNTESS *(softly)*
If I survive this storm
I'll fear no further shipwreck.

FIGARO *(softly)*
In vain he fumes and stamps;
poor thing, I am smarter than him.

Scene XII

The above, Marcellina, Bartolo and Basilio

MARCELLINA, BASILIO and BARTOLO *(entering, to the Count)*
Oh my just and noble lord, [31]
Hear us now, we pray.

COUNT *(aside)*
They've come to work my vengeance.
I feel consoled.

SUSANNA, COUNTESS and FIGARO *(aside)*
They've come to foil me.
What solution can there be?

FIGARO *(to the Count)*
They're three stupid blockheads.
What are they doing here?

COUNT
Now quiet: without interruption
let each say what he wishes.

MARCELLINA
This man has made a contract
promising to marry me;
and I request that the contract
shall be ratified.

SUSANNA, LA CONTESSA e FIGARO
Come! Come!

IL CONTE
Olà, silenzio!
Io son qui per giudicar.

BARTOLO
Io da lei scelto avvocato
vengo a far le sue difese,
le legittime pretese,
io qui vengo a palesar.

SUSANNA, LA CONTESSA e FIGARO
È un birbante!

IL CONTE
Olà, silenzio!
Io son qui per giudicar.

BASILIO
Io, com'uom al mondo cognito
vengo qui per testimonio
del promesso matrimonio
con prestanza di danar.

SUSANNA, LA CONTESSA e FIGARO
Son tre matti.

IL CONTE
Lo vedremo,
il contratto leggeremo.
Tutto in ordin deve andar.

SUSANNA e LA CONTESSA
Son confusa, son stordita,
disperata, sbalordita.
Certo un diavol dell'inferno
qui li ha fatti capitar.

SUSANNA, COUNTESS and FIGARO
What's this?

COUNT
Keep quiet, there.
This is for me to judge.

BARTOLO
I represent this lady
and appear here as her counsel;
I come to argue
her legitimate plea.

SUSANNA, COUNTESS and FIGARO
He's a rogue!

COUNT
Keep quiet, there.
This is for me to judge.

BASILIO
As a man of standing,
I come here as a witness
of the promised marriage,
on which she lent him money.

SUSANNA, COUNTESS and FIGARO
They're really mad.

COUNT
Let's see it,
let us read the contract.
Everything must be done in proper order.

SUSANNA and COUNTESS
I'm stunned and bewildered,
stupefied and desperate!
The Devil in hell for certain
has brought them here.

FIGARO
Son confuso, son stordito,
disperato, sbalordito.
Certo un diavol dell'inferno
qui li ha fatti capitar.

MARCELLINA, BASILIO e BARTOLO
Che bel colpo, che bel caso!
È cresciuto a tutti il naso;
qualche nume a noi propizio
qui ci ha fatti capitar.

IL CONTE
Che bel colpo, che bel caso!
È cresciuto a tutti il naso,
qualche nume a noi propizio
qui li ha fatti capitar.

FIGARO
I'm stunned and bewildered,
stupefied and desperate!
The Devil in hell for certain
has brought them here.

MARCELLINA, BASILIO and BARTOLO
What a blow, what a splendid stroke!
Everyone is baffled;
Providence, that smiles on us,
has brought us here.

COUNT
What a blow, what a splendid stroke!
Everyone is baffled;
Providence, that smiles on us,
has brought us here.

ATTO TERZO

Scena I

Sala ricca con due troni e preparata a festa nuziale. Il Conte solo.

Recitativo

IL CONTE *(passeggiando)*
Che imbarazzo è mai questo! Un foglio anonimo...
La cameriera in gabinetto chiusa...
La padrona confusa... un uom che salta
dal balcone in giardino... un altro appresso
che dice esser quel desso...
Non so cosa pensar. Potrebbe forse
qualcun de' miei vassalli... a simil razza
è comune l'ardir, ma la Contessa...
Ah, che un dubbio l'offende. Ella rispetta
troppo sé stessa; e l'onor mio... l'onore...
Dove diamin l'ha posto umano errore!

Scena II

Il suddetto, la Contessa e Susanna; s'arrestano in fondo alla scena, non vedute dal Conte.

LA CONTESSA *(a Susanna)*
Via, fatti core: digli
che ti attenda in giardino.

IL CONTE *(tra sé)*
Saprò se Cherubino
era giunto a Siviglia. A tale oggetto
ho mandato Basilio...

SUSANNA *(alla Contessa)*
Oh cielo! E Figaro?

LA CONTESSA
A lui non déi dir nulla: in vece tua
voglio andarci io medesma.

ACT THREE

Scene I

A rich hall with two thrones, prepared for the wedding. The Count alone.

Recitative

COUNT *(pacing up and down)*
What a mix-up this is! An anonymous letter...
The maid locked in the dressing room...
My lady flustered... a man jumping down
from the balcony into the garden...then another
who claims it was he...
I don't know what to think: it might
have been one of my vassals... such rabble
are bold enough... but the Countess...
No, to doubt her is an insult... She has too much
respect for herself; and for my honour... my honour...
What has human weakness done to it!

Scene II

Enter the Countess and Susanna; they stay in the background, unseen by the Count.

COUNTESS *(to Susanna)*
Go on, take courage: tell him
to meet you in the garden.

COUNT *(aside)*
I'll find out if Cherubino
went to Seville: I've sent
Basilio to enquire...

SUSANNA *(to the Countess)*
Oh Heavens! And Figaro?

COUNTESS
Say nothing of it to him: I myself
intend going in your place.

IL CONTE

Avanti sera

dovrebbe ritornar…

SUSANNA

Oh Dio… non oso!

LA CONTESSA

Pensa ch'è in tua mano il mio riposo.

(Si nasconde.)

IL CONTE

E Susanna? Chi sa ch'ella tradito
abbia il segreto mio… oh, se ha parlato,
gli fo sposar la vecchia.

SUSANNA *(piano)*

Marcellina!

(al Conte)

Signor…

IL CONTE

Cosa bramate?

SUSANNA

Mi par che siate in collera!

IL CONTE

Volete qualche cosa?

SUSANNA

Signor… la vostra sposa
ha i soliti vapori,
e vi chiede il fiaschetto degli odori.

IL CONTE

Prendete.

SUSANNA

Or vel riporto.

COUNT

Before this evening

he should be back...

SUSANNA

Oh Lord! I dare not.

COUNTESS

Reflect that my happiness is in your hands.

(She hides.)

COUNT

And Susanna? Who knows if she
has betrayed my secret?... If she's spoken,
I'll make him marry the old woman.

SUSANNA *(softly)*

Marcellina!

(to the Count)

My lord...

COUNT

What do you want?

SUSANNA

I believe you're angry!

COUNT

What have you come for?

SUSANNA

My lord... my lady
has the vapours, as usual,
and requests your smelling salts.

COUNT

Take them.

SUSANNA

I'll bring them back at once.

IL CONTE
Ah no, potete
ritenerlo per voi.

SUSANNA
Per me?
Questi non sono mali
da donne triviali.

IL CONTE
Un'amante che perde il caro sposo
sul punto d'ottenerlo.

SUSANNA
Pagando Marcellina
colla dote che voi mi prometteste...

IL CONTE
Ch'io vi promisi, quando?

SUSANNA
Credea d'averlo inteso.

IL CONTE
Sì, se voluto aveste
intendermi voi stessa.

SUSANNA
È mio dovere,
e quel di Sua Eccellenza il mio volere.

N°16 Duettino

IL CONTE
Crudel! Perché finora [32]
farmi languir così?

SUSANNA
Signor, la donna ognora
tempo ha dir di sì.

IL CONTE
Dunque, in giardin verrai?

COUNT

No, you may keep them

for yourself.

SUSANNA

For me?
Such ailments are not
for girls in my position.

COUNT

A girl who loses her bridegroom
on the point of winning him...

SUSANNA

Paying Marcellina off
with the dowry you promised me...

COUNT

That I promised you? When?

SUSANNA

That's what I understood.

COUNT

Yes, if you had cared
to come to an understanding.

SUSANNA

It's my duty,

and my lord's wish is my command.

No. 16 Duet

COUNT

Cruel one, why have you [32]
caused me thus to languish?

SUSANNA

My lord, a woman always
needs time before she says 'Yes'.

COUNT

Then you'll come into the garden?

SUSANNA
Se piace a voi, verrò.

IL CONTE
E non mi mancherai?

SUSANNA
No, non vi mancherò.

IL CONTE
Mi sento dal contento [33]
pieno di gioia il cor.

SUSANNA *(piano)*
Scusatemi se mento,
voi che intendete amor.

Recitativo

IL CONTE
E perché fosti meco
stamattina sì austera?

SUSANNA
Col paggio ch'ivi c'era...

IL CONTE
Ed a Basilio
che per me ti parlò...

SUSANNA
Ma qual bisogno
abbiam noi, che un Basilio...

IL CONTE
È vero, è vero,
e mi prometti poi...
se tu manchi, oh cor mio... Ma la Contessa
attenderà il fiaschetto.

SUSANNA
Eh, fu un pretesto.
Parlato io non avrei senza di questo.

SUSANNA
If it pleases you, I'll come.

COUNT
You won't fail me?

SUSANNA
No, I won't fail you.

COUNT
In contentment I feel [33]
my heart full of joy.

SUSANNA *(aside)*
Forgive my deception,
you who truly love.

Recitative

COUNT
Then why were you
so distant to me this morning?

SUSANNA
With the page there…

COUNT
And to Basilio,
who spoke on my behalf…

SUSANNA
But what need have we
of a Basilio…

COUNT
That's true, indeed.
Promise me again…
If you fail me, my dear… But the Countess
will be waiting for the smelling salts.

SUSANNA
Oh, that was just a pretext;
I couldn't have spoken to you without one.

IL CONTE *(le prende la mano)*
Carissima!

SUSANNA *(si ritira)*
Vien gente.

IL CONTE *(tra sé)*
È mia senz'altro.

SUSANNA *(tra sé)*
Forbitevi la bocca, oh signor scaltro.

(Vuol partire, e sotto la porta s'incontra in Figaro.)

Scena III

Figaro, Susanna ed il Conte.

FIGARO
Ehi, Susanna, ove vai?

SUSANNA
Taci, senza avvocato
hai già vinta la causa.

(parte)

FIGARO
Cos'è nato?

(La segue.)

Scena IV

Il Conte solo.

N°17 *Recitativo ed Aria*

IL CONTE
Hai già vinta la causa! Cosa sento!
In qual laccio io cadea? Perfidi! Io voglio
di tal modo punirvi... A piacer mio
la sentenza sarà... Ma s'ei pagasse
la vecchia pretendente?

COUNT *(taking her hand)*
Dearest!

SUSANNA *(withdrawing)*
Someone's coming.

COUNT *(aside)*
She's mine, I'm sure now.

SUSANNA *(aside)*
Wipe off that smile, my cunning master.

(She is about to leave and near the door meets Figaro.)

Scene III

Figaro, Susanna and the Count.

FIGARO
Susanna, where are you going?

SUSANNA
Hush. You've won your case
without a lawyer.

(exit)

FIGARO
What's happened?

(He follows her.)

Scene IV

The Count alone.

No. 17 Recitative and Aria

COUNT
You've won your case! What do I hear!
I've fallen into a trap! The traitors!
I'll punish them so! The sentence
will be at my pleasure… But supposing
he has paid off the claims of the old woman?

Pagarla! In qual maniera! E poi v'è Antonio,
che a un incognito Figaro ricusa
di dare una nipote in matrimonio.
Coltivando l'orgoglio
di questo mentecatto…
Tutto giova a un raggiro… il colpo è fatto.

Vedrò, mentre io sospiro, [34]
felice un servo mio?
E un ben ch'invan desio
ei posseder dovrà?
Vedrò per man d'amore
unita a un vile oggetto
chi in me destò un affetto
che per me poi non ha?
Ah no, lasciarti in pace,
non vo' questo contento,
tu non nascesti, audace,
per dare a me tormento,
e forse ancor per ridere
di mia infelicità!
Già la speranza sola [35]
delle vendette mie
quest'anima consola,
e giubilar mi fa.

(Vuol partire, e s'incontra in Don Curzio.)

Scena V

Il Conte, Marcellina, Don Curzio, Figaro e Bartolo; poi Susanna.

Recitativo

DON CURZIO
È decisa la lite.
'O pagarla, o sposarla.' Ora ammutite.

MARCELLINA
Io respiro.

Paid her? How?... And then there's Antonio,
who'll refuse to give his niece in marriage
to a Figaro, of whom nothing is known.
If I play on the pride
of that half-wit...
Everything favours my plan... The die is cast.

Must I see a serf of mine made happy [34]
while I am left to sigh,
and him possess a treasure
which I desire in vain?
Must I see her,
who has roused in me a passion
she does not feel for me,
united by the hand of love to a base slave?
Ah no, I will not give you
the satisfaction of this contentment!
You were not born, bold fellow,
to cause me torment
and indeed to laugh
at my discomfiture!
Now only the hope [35]
of taking vengeance
eases my mind
and makes me rejoice.

(As he is leaving, he meets Don Curzio.)

Scene V

The Count, Marcellina, Don Curzio, Figaro and Bartolo; then Susanna.

Recitative

DON CURZIO
The case is decided.
'Pay up, or marry her.' That's all.

MARCELLINA
I breathe again.

FIGARO

Ed io moro.

MARCELLINA *(tra sé)*

Alfin sposa io sarò d'un uom ch'adoro.

FIGARO *(al Conte)*

Eccellenza m'appello…

IL CONTE

È giusta la sentenza.
'O pagar, o sposar.' Bravo Don Curzio.

DON CURZIO

Bontà di sua Eccellenza.

BARTOLO

Che superba sentenza!

FIGARO

In che superba?

BARTOLO

Siam tutti vendicati…

FIGARO

Io non la sposerò.

BARTOLO

La sposerai.

DON CURZIO

'O pagarla, o sposarla.' Lei t'ha prestati
due mille pezzi duri.

FIGARO

Son gentiluomo, e senza
l'assenso de' miei nobili parenti…

IL CONTE

Dove sono? Chi sono?

FIGARO

And I'm done for.

MARCELLINA *(aside)*

At last I'll be married to the man I love.

FIGARO *(to the Count)*

My lord, I appeal…

COUNT

The judgement is fair:
'Pay up, or marry her.' Quite right, Don Curzio.

DON CURZIO

Your lordship is too kind.

BARTOLO

An excellent judgement!

FIGARO

In what way excellent?

BARTOLO

We are all avenged.

FIGARO

I won't marry her.

BARTOLO

Oh yes, you will.

DON CURZIO

'Pay up, or marry her.' She lent you
two thousand pieces of silver.

FIGARO

I am of gentle birth, and without
the consent of my noble parents…

COUNT

Where are they? Who are they?

FIGARO
Lasciate ancor cercarli!
Dopo dieci anni io spero di trovarli.

BARTOLO
Qualche bambin trovato?

FIGARO
No, perduto, dottor, anzi rubato.

IL CONTE
Come?

MARCELLINA
Cosa?

BARTOLO
La prova?

DON CURZIO
Il testimonio?

FIGARO
L'oro, le gemme, e i ricamati panni
che ne' più teneri anni
mi ritrovaro addosso i masnadieri
sono gl'indizi veri
di mia nascita illustre, e sopra tutto
questo al mio braccio impresso geroglifico…

MARCELLINA
Una spatola impressa al braccio destro…

FIGARO
E a voi chi'l disse?

MARCELLINA
Oh Dio
È egli…

FIGARO
È ver, son io.

FIGARO
Let me go on looking for them;
for ten years I've been hoping to find them.

BARTOLO
Were you a foundling?...

FIGARO
No, lost, doctor, or rather stolen.

COUNT
Stolen?

MARCELLINA
What's that?

BARTOLO
Your proof?

DON CURZIO
Your witness?

FIGARO
The gold, the jewels and the embroidered clothes
which, in my infancy,
the bandits found upon me
are the true indications
of my noble birth, and moreover
this mark upon my arm.

MARCELLINA
A spatula on your right arm?

FIGARO
Who told you that?

MARCELLINA
Great Heaven!
It's he...

FIGARO
It's I, indeed.

DON CURZIO
Chi?

IL CONTE
Chi?

BARTOLO
Chi?

MARCELLINA
Raffaello.

BARTOLO
E i ladri ti rapir…

FIGARO
Presso un castello.

BARTOLO
Ecco tua madre.

FIGARO
Balia?…

BARTOLO
No, tua madre.

IL CONTE e DON CURZIO
Sua madre!

FIGARO
Cosa sento!

MARCELLINA
Ecco tuo padre.

(Corre ad abbracciare Figaro.)

N°18 Sestetto

MARCELLINA *(abbracciando Figaro)*
Riconosci in questo amplesso [36]
una madre, amato figlio!

DON CURZIO
Who?

COUNT
Who?

BARTOLO
Who?

MARCELLINA
Raffaello.

BARTOLO
And some robbers stole you…

FIGARO
Near a castle.

BARTOLO
There stands your mother.

FIGARO
My nurse?…

BARTOLO
No, your mother.

COUNT and DON CURZIO
His mother!

FIGARO
Do I hear rightly?

MARCELLINA
And there stands your father.

(She runs to embrace Figaro.)

No. 18 Sextet

MARCELLINA *(embracing Figaro)*
Dearest son, in this embrace [36]
recognize your mother.

FIGARO *(a Bartolo)*
Padre mio, fate lo stesso,
non mi fate più arrossir.

BARTOLO *(abbracciando Figaro)*
Resistenza la coscienza
far non lascia al tuo desir.

DON CURZIO *(tra sé)*
Ei suo padre, ella sua madre,
l'imeneo non può seguir.

IL CONTE *(tra sé)*
Son smarrito, son stordito,
meglio è assai di qua partir.

MARCELLINA e BARTOLO
Figlio amato!

FIGARO
Parenti amati!

(Il Conte vuol partire. Susanna entra con una borsa in mano.)

SUSANNA
Alto, alto, signor Conte,
mille doppie son qui pronte,
a pagar vengo per Figaro,
ed a porlo in libertà.

IL CONTE e DON CURZIO
Non sappiam com'è la cosa,
osservate un poco là!

SUSANNA *(si volge e vede Figaro che abbraccia Marcellina)*
Già d'accordo ei colla sposa;
giusti Dei, che infedeltà!

(vuol partire)

Lascia, iniquo!

FIGARO *(to Bartolo)*
Father dear, do the same,
do not leave me longer here to blush.

BARTOLO *(embracing Figaro)*
Do not let conscience
stand in the way of your desire.

DON CURZIO *(aside)*
He's his father, she's his mother:
the wedding can't go forward.

COUNT *(aside)*
I'm astounded, I'm amazed:
to leave here would be for the best.

MARCELLINA and BARTOLO
Beloved son!

FIGARO
Beloved parents!

(The Count makes to leave. Enter Susanna with a purse in her hand.)

SUSANNA
Just a moment, pray, my lord.
I have the money ready here.
I've come to pay for Figaro
and set him free.

COUNT and DON CURZIO
We don't know where we are.
Just look over there.

SUSANNA *(turning and seeing Figaro embrace Marcellina)*
Already reconciled to her as wife?
Great Heaven, how faithless!

(about to leave)

Leave me, wretch!

FIGARO *(trattenendo Susanna)*
No, t'arresta!
Senti, oh cara!

SUSANNA *(dà uno schiaffo a Figaro)*
Senti questa!

MARCELLINA, BARTOLO e FIGARO
È un effetto di buon core,
tutto amore è quel che fa.

IL CONTE
Fremo, smanio dal furore,
il destino a me la fa.

DON CURZIO
Freme e smania dal furore,
il destino gliela fa.

SUSANNA
Fremo, smanio dal furore,
una vecchia me la fa.

MARCELLINA *(corre ad abbracciar Susanna)*
Lo sdegno calmate,
mia cara figliuola,
sua madre abbracciate
che or vostra sarà.

SUSANNA
Sua madre? [37]

TUTTI
Sua madre!

FIGARO
E quello è mio padre
che a te lo dirà.

SUSANNA
Suo padre?

FIGARO *(holding her back)*
Stay a moment.
Listen, my dearest.

SUSANNA *(boxing Figaro's ears)*
Listen to that!

MARCELLINA, BARTOLO and FIGARO
It's the result of her full heart;
what she did, she did for love.

COUNT
I rage, I burn with fury;
fate has overcome me.

DON CURZIO
He rages, he burns with fury;
fate has overcome him.

SUSANNA
I rage, I burn with fury;
this old woman has overcome me.

MARCELLINA *(running to embrace Susanna)*
Dearest daughter,
calm your bitterness,
and embrace his mother,
who now will be yours too.

SUSANNA
His mother? [37]

ALL
His mother.

FIGARO
And this is my father,
who'll tell you it's true.

SUSANNA
His father?

TUTTI

Suo padre!

FIGARO

E quella è mia madre
che a te lo dirà.

(Corrono tutti quattro ad abbracciarsi.)

SUSANNA, MARCELLINA, BARTOLO e FIGARO

Al dolce contento
di questo momento,
quest'anima appena
resister or sa.

DON CURZIO ed IL CONTE

Al fiero tormento
di questo momento,
quest'anima appena
resister or sa.

(Il Conte e Don Curzio partono.)

Scena VI

Susanna, Marcellina, Figaro e Bartolo.

Recitativo

MARCELLINA *(a Bartolo)*

Eccovi, oh caro amico, il dolce frutto
dell'antico amor nostro...

BARTOLO

Or non parliamo
di fatti sì rimoti: egli è mio figlio,
mia consorte voi siete;
e le nozze farem quando volete.

MARCELLINA

Oggi, e doppie saranno.

(dà il biglietto a Figaro)

ALL
His father.

FIGARO
And this is my mother,
who'll tell you it's true.

(All four embrace.)

SUSANNA, MARCELLINA, BARTOLO and FIGARO
My heart
scarcely can support
the bliss
of this moment.

COUNT and DON CURZIO
My heart
scarcely can support
the raging torment
of this moment.

(The Count and Don Curzio exeunt.)

Scene VI

Susanna, Marcellina, Figaro and Bartolo.

Recitative

MARCELLINA *(to Bartolo)*
And there, my dear, is the sweet pledge
of our old love...

BARTOLO
Let's not talk now
of so remote a past: he's my son,
you are my consort;
and we'll get married when you wish.

MARCELLINA
Today; it can be a double wedding.

(giving the paper to Figaro)

Prendi, questo è il biglietto
del danar che a me devi, ed è tua dote.

SUSANNA *(getta per terra una borsa di danari)*
Prendi ancor questa borsa.

BARTOLO *(fa lo stesso)*
E questa ancora.

FIGARO
Bravi, gittate pur, ch'io piglio ognora.

SUSANNA
Voliamo ad informar d'ogni avventura
madama e nostro zio.
Chi al par di me contenta!

FIGARO
Io!

BARTOLO
Io!

MARCELLINA
Io!

TUTTI
E schiatti il signor Conte al gusto mio.

(Partono abbracciati.)

Scena VII

Barbarina e Cherubino.

Recitativo

BARBARINA
Andiam, andiam, bel paggio, in casa mia
tutte ritroverai
le più belle ragazze del castello,
di tutte sarai tu certo il più bello.

Take this; it is the contract for the sum
you owe me; let it be your wedding present.

SUSANNA *(throwing down a purse of money)*
Take this purse too.

BARTOLO *(doing the same)*
And this as well.

FIGARO
Thank you; I'll take all I'm given.

SUSANNA
Let's go and tell my lady
and my uncle all that's happened;
who could be as happy as I am?

FIGARO
I am.

BARTOLO
I am.

MARCELLINA
I am.

ALL
And I don't care how furious the Count is!

(Exeunt arm in arm.)

Scene VII

Barbarina and Cherubino.

Recitativo

BARBARINA
Come, dear page, come to our house.
Here you'll find
all the prettiest girls of the estate.
And you shall be the prettiest of them all.

CHERUBINO
Ah, se il Conte mi trova,
misero me! Tu sai
che partito ei mi crede per Siviglia.

BARBARINA
Oh ve' che maraviglia, e se ti trova,
non sarà cosa nuova...
Odi, vogliam vestirti come noi:
tutte insiem andrem poi
a presentar de' fiori a madamina.
Fìdati, o Cherubin, di Barbarina.

(partono)

Scena VIII

La Contessa sola.

N°19 Recitativo ed Aria

LA CONTESSA
E Susanna non vien! Son ansiosa
di saper come il Conte
accolse la proposta. Alquanto ardito
il progetto mi par, e ad uno sposo
sì vivace e geloso!
Ma che mal c'è? Cangiando i miei vestiti
con quelli di Susanna, e i suoi co' miei...
Al favor della notte... oh cielo, a quale
umil stato fatale io son ridotta
da un consorte crudel, che dopo avermi
con un misto inaudito
d'infedeltà, di gelosia, di sdegni,
prima amata, indi offesa e alfin tradita,
fammi or cercar da una mia serva aita!

Dove sono i bei momenti [38]
di dolcezza e di piacer,
dove andaro i giuramenti
di quel labbro menzogner?

CHERUBINO
But woe betide me if the Count
should find me! You know
he thinks I've left for Seville.

BARBARINA
Oh well, if he does find you,
it won't be anything new.
Listen, we're going to dress you like one of us,
and then all go
to present flowers to my lady.
Cherubino, have faith in Barbarina.

(exeunt)

Scene VIII

The Countess, alone.

No. 19 Recitative and Aria

COUNTESS
Susanna's not come! I'm impatient
to know what the Count said
to her proposal; the plan seems to me
somewhat rash, and with a husband
so impetuous and jealous...
But where's the harm? To change my clothes
with those of Susanna, and hers with mine...
Under cover of darkness... Oh Heavens!
To what humiliation am I reduced
by a cruel husband, who after having
first loved me, then neglected and finally
deceived me, in a strange mixture
of infidelity, jealousy and disdain,
now forces me to seek help from my servant!

Where are those happy moments [38]
of sweetness and pleasure?
Where have they gone,
those vows of a deceiving tongue?

Perché mai se in pianti e in pene
per me tutto si cangiò,
la memoria di quel bene
dal mio sen non trapassò?
Ah! Se almen la mia costanza
nel languire amando ognor,
mi portasse una speranza
di cangiar l'ingrato cor.

(parte)

Scena IX

Il Conte ed Antonio.

Recitativo

ANTONIO *(con un cappello in mano)*
Io vi dico, signor, che Cherubino
è ancora nel castello,
e vedete per prova il suo cappello.

IL CONTE
Ma come, se a quest'ora
esser giunto a Siviglia egli dovria.

ANTONIO
Scusate, oggi Siviglia è a casa mia.
Là vestissi da donna, e là lasciati
ha gli altri abiti suoi.

IL CONTE
Perfidi!

ANTONIO
Andiam, e li vedrete voi.

(partono)

Then why, if everything for me
is changed to tears and grief,
has the memory of that happiness
not faded from my breast?
Ah! if only my constancy
in yearning lovingly for him always
could bring the hope
of changing his ungrateful heart!

(exit)

Scene IX

Enter the Count and Antonio.

Recitative

ANTONIO *(with a cap in his hand)*
I tell you, sir, that Cherubino
is still in the castle;
look, here's his cap to prove it.

COUNT
But how? By this time
he ought to be in Seville.

ANTONIO
If I may say so, all Seville's in my house.
There he's been dressed as a girl,
and he's left his other clothes there.

COUNT
The traitors!

ANTONIO
Let's go, and you can see for yourself.

(exeunt)

Scena X

La Contessa e Susanna.

Recitativo

LA CONTESSA
Cosa mi narri, e che ne disse il Conte?

SUSANNA
Gli si leggeva in fronte
il dispetto e la rabbia.

LA CONTESSA
Piano, che meglio or lo porremo in gabbia.
Dov'è l'appuntamento
che tu gli proponesti?

SUSANNA
In giardino.

LA CONTESSA
Fissiamgli un loco. Scrivi.

SUSANNA
Ch'io scriva… Ma, signora…

LA CONTESSA
Eh, scrivi dico; e tutto
io prendo su me stessa.

(Susanna siede e scrive.)

'Canzonetta sull'aria…'

SUSANNA *(scrivendo)*
Sull'aria…

N°20 Duettino

LA CONTESSA *(detta)*
'Che soave zeffiretto…' [39]

Scene X

The Countess and Susanna.

Recitative

COUNTESS
What are you saying? And what did the Count say then?

SUSANNA
You could read in his face
his indignation and anger.

COUNTESS
Gently now: it will be the easier to catch him.
Where is the rendezvous
that you suggested?

SUSANNA
In the garden.

COUNTESS
Let's fix a place for it. Write to him.

SUSANNA
I write?... But... my lady...

COUNTESS
Write, I tell you,
and I'll take it all upon myself.

(Susanna sits down and writes)

A song to the breezes...

SUSANNA *(writing)*
To the breezes...

No. 20 Duet

COUNTESS *(dictating)*
'How sweet the zephyr...' [39]

SUSANNA *(ripete le parole della Contessa)*
Zeffiretto...

LA CONTESSA
'Questa sera spirerà...'

SUSANNA
Questa sera spirerà...

LA CONTESSA
'Sotto i pini del boschetto.'

SUSANNA *(domandando)*
Sotto i pini?

LA CONTESSA
'Sotto i pini del boschetto.'

SUSANNA *(scrivendo)*
Sotto i pini del boschetto...

LA CONTESSA
Ei già il resto capirà.

SUSANNA
Certo, certo il capirà.

(Rileggono insieme lo scritto.)

Recitativo

SUSANNA *(piega la lettera)*
Piegato è il foglio... or come si sigilla?

LA CONTESSA *(si cava una spilla e gliela dà)*
Ecco... prendi una spilla:
Servirà di sigillo. Attendi... scrivi
sul riverso del foglio,
'Rimandate il sigillo'.

SUSANNA
È più bizzarro
di quel della patente.

SUSANNA *(repeating the Countess's words)*
The zephyr...

COUNTESS
'Will be this evening...'

SUSANNA
Will be this evening...

COUNTESS
'In the pine grove.'

SUSANNA *(questioning)*
In the pine grove?

LA CONTESSA
'In the pine grove.'

SUSANNA *(writing)*
In the pine grove.

COUNTESS
The rest he'll understand.

SUSANNA
I'm sure he'll understand.

(Together they reread what has been written.)

Recitative

SUSANNA *(folds the letter)*
The letter's folded... how shall I seal it?

COUNTESS *(taking out a pin and giving it to her)*
Here... take this pin.
It will serve as seal. Wait... write
on the back of the letter,
'Send back the seal'.

SUSANNA
It's stranger than
the seal on the commission.

LA CONTESSA
Presto nascondi, io sento venir gente.

(Susanna si pone il biglietto nel seno.)

Scena XI

Cherubino vestito da contadinella, Barbarina e alcune altre contadinelle vestite nel medesimo modo con mazzetti di fiori e i suddetti.

N°21 Coro

CONTADINELLE
Ricevete, o padroncina, [40]
queste rose e questi fior,
che abbiam colti stamattina
per mostrarvi il nostro amor.
Siamo tante contadine,
e siam tutte poverine,
ma quel poco che rechiamo
ve lo diamo di buon cor.

Recitativo

BARBARINA
Queste sono, madama,
le ragazze del loco
che il poco ch'han vi vengono ad offrire,
e vi chiedon perdon del loro ardire.

LA CONTESSA
Oh brave, vi ringrazio.

SUSANNA
Come sono vezzose!

LA CONTESSA *(indica Cherubino)*
E chi è, narratemi,
quell'amabil fanciulla
ch'ha l'aria sì modesta?

COUNTESS
Quick, hide it… I hear people coming.

(Susanna puts the note in her bosom.)

Scene XI

Enter Cherubino dressed as a peasant girl, Barbarina, and other village girls dressed in the same way, with bunches of flowers.

No. 21 Chorus

PEASANT GIRLS
Accept, noble lady, [40]
these roses and these flowers,
which we have picked this morning
to show you our affection.
We are only humble girls
from the village,
but the little that we can give
we offer with all our hearts.

Recitative

BARBARINA
These, my lady,
are the girls of the district,
who have come to offer what little they have
and beg your pardon for being so bold.

COUNTESS
How kind! I thank you.

SUSANNA
Aren't they pretty!

COUNTESS *(indicating Cherubino)*
And who, tell me,
is that charming girl
who looks so shy?

BARBARINA
Ell'è una mia cugina, e per le nozze
è venuta ier sera.

LA CONTESSA
Onoriamo la bella forestiera.

(to Cherubino)

Venite qui… datemi i vostri fiori.

(prende i fiori di Cherubino e lo bacia in fronte; tra sé)

Come arrossì!

(to Susanna)

Susanna, e non ti pare…
che somigli ad alcuno?

SUSANNA
Al naturale.

Scena XII

I suddetti, il Conte ed Antonio. Questi ha il cappello di Cherubino: entra in scena pian piano, gli cava la cuffia di donna e gli mette in testa il cappello stesso.

ANTONIO
Ehi! Cospettaccio! È questi l'uffiziale.

LA CONTESSA *(tra sé)*
Oh stelle!

SUSANNA *(tra sé)*
Malandrino!

IL CONTE *(alla Contessa)*
Ebben, madama…

LA CONTESSA
Io sono, oh signor mio,
irritata e sorpresa al par di voi.

BARBARINA
That's one of my cousins, who came
yesterday evening for the wedding.

COUNTESS
We should honour this fair stranger.

(to Cherubino)

Come here… let me have your flowers.

(taking the flowers from Cherubino and kissing his forehead; aside)

How she blushes!

(to Susanna)

Susanna, don't you think…
she resembles someone?

SUSANNA
To the life!

Scene XII

Enter the Count and Antonio. Antonio, holding Cherubino's cap, enters very quietly, pulls off Cherubino's headdress and puts the cap on him.

ANTONIO
There you are! There's your officer!

COUNTESS *(aside)*
Mercy on us!

SUSANNA *(aside)*
The scamp!

COUNT *(to the Countess)*
Well, madam?…

COUNTESS
My lord, I am as annoyed
and surprised as you are.

IL CONTE
Ma stamane?

LA CONTESSA
Stamane...
Per l'odierna festa
volevam travestirlo al modo stesso
che l'han vestito adesso.

IL CONTE *(a Cherubino)*
E perché non partiste?

CHERUBINO *(cavandosi il cappello bruscamente)*
Signor...

IL CONTE
Saprò punire
la sua disubbidienza.

BARBARINA
Eccellenza, Eccellenza,
voi mi dite sì spesso,
qual volta m'abbracciate e mi baciate:
'Barbarina, se m'ami,
ti darò quel che brami...'

IL CONTE
Io dissi questo?

BARBARINA
Voi.
Or datemi, padrone,
in sposo Cherubino,
e v'amerò com'amo il mio gattino.

LA CONTESSA *(al Conte)*
Ebbene: or tocca a voi.

ANTONIO *(a Barbarina)*
Brava figliuola,
hai buon maestro che ti fa la scola.

COUNT
But this morning?

COUNTESS
This morning…
We wanted to dress him up
as he's dressed now
for this evening's party.

COUNT *(to Cherubino)*
And why have you not left?

CHERUBINO *(quickly pulling off his cap)*
My lord…

COUNT
I shall know
how to punish your disobedience.

BARBARINA
Your lordship, your lordship,
you've told me so often,
when you've kissed and caressed me,
'Barbarina, if you'll love me,
I'll give you whatever you want…'

COUNT
I said that?

BARBARINA
Yes, you did.
So please give me, sir,
Cherubino for a husband,
and I'll love you as I love my kitten.

COUNTESS *(to the Count)*
Well, now it's your turn…

ANTONIO *(to Barbarina)*
Well done, my girl!
You've learnt your lesson well.

IL CONTE *(tra sé)*
Non so qual uom, qual demone, qual Dio
rivolga tutto quanto a torto mio.

Scena XIII

I suddetti e Figaro

FIGARO
Signor… se trattenete
tutte queste ragazze,
addio feste… addio danza…

IL CONTE
E che, vorresti
ballar col piè stravolto?

FIGARO *(finge di drizzarsi la gamba e poi si prova a ballare)*
Eh, non mi duol più molto.
Andiam, belle fanciulle.

(Chiama tutte le giovani, vuol partire; il Conte lo richiama.)

LA CONTESSA *(a Susanna)*
Come si caverà dall'imbarazzo?

SUSANNA *(alla Contessa)*
Lasciate fare a lui.

IL CONTE
Per buona sorte
i vasi eran di creta.

FIGARO
Senza fallo.
Andiamo dunque, andiamo.

(Vuol partire; Antonio lo richiama.)

ANTONIO
E intanto a cavallo
di galoppo a Siviglia andava il paggio.

COUNT *(aside)*
What man, demon or god is it
that turns everything I do against me?

Scene XIII

The above. Enter Figaro.

FIGARO
My lord… if you keep
all these girls here,
there'll be no party, no dancing…

COUNT
Indeed! You're wanting
to dance with an injured foot?

FIGARO *(pretending to stretch his leg and then trying to dance)*
Oh, it doesn't hurt any more.
Come, my pretty ones…

(He calls all the girls and tries to leave, but the Count calls him back.)

COUNTESS *(to Susanna)*
How will he manage to escape now?

SUSANNA *(to the Countess)*
Be sure he'll do it.

COUNT
By good fortune,
the flower pots were only earthenware.

FIGARO
That's right.
Come along now, come along…

(He tries to leave, but Antonio calls him back.)

ANTONIO
Meanwhile the page
was galloping off to Seville?

FIGARO
Di galoppo, o di passo... buon viaggio.

(per partire)

Venite, belle giovani.

IL CONTE *(torna a ricondurlo in mezzo)*
E a te la sua patente
era in tasca rimasta...

FIGARO
Certamente.
Che razza di domande!

ANTONIO *(a Susanna, che fa de' motti a Figaro)*
Via, non gli far più motti, ei non t'intende.

(prende per mano Cherubino e lo presenta a Figaro)

Ed ecco chi pretende
che sia un bugiardo il mio signor nipote.

FIGARO
Cherubino!

ANTONIO
Or ci sei.

FIGARO *(al Conte)*
Che diamin canta?

IL CONTE
Non canta, no, ma dice
ch'egli saltò stamane sui garofani...

FIGARO
Ei lo dice! Sarà... se ho saltato io,
si può dare che anch'esso
abbia fatto lo stesso.

IL CONTE
Anch'esso?

FIGARO
Galloping or trotting, off he went.

(about to leave)

Come along, my dears.

COUNT *(again bringing him back)*
And his commission
was left in your pocket…

FIGARO
Yes indeed.
What sort of questions!

ANTONIO *(to Susanna, who is making signs to Figaro)*
Stop making signs to him, he doesn't understand.

(taking Cherubino by the hand and presenting him to Figaro)

Here's someone who claims
that my nephew-to-be is a liar.

FIGARO
Cherubino!

ANTONIO
There you are.

FIGARO *(to the Count)*
What's this story of his?

COUNT
No story; but he says it was he
who jumped on the carnations this morning…

FIGARO
He says so!… Well, if I jumped down,
it's possible that he too
could have done the same.

COUNT
He too?

FIGARO

Perché no?
Io non impugno mai quel che non so.

(S'ode la marcia da lontano.)

N°22 *Finale* [41]

FIGARO
Ecco la marcia, andiamo…
A' vostri posti, o belle, ai vostri posti.
Susanna, dammi il braccio.

SUSANNA
Eccolo!

(Figaro prende per un braccio Antonio, per l'altro Susanna, e partono tutti eccettuati il Conte e la Contessa.)

IL CONTE *(tra sé)*
Temerari.

LA CONTESSA *(tra sé)*
Io son di ghiaccio!

IL CONTE
Contessa…

LA CONTESSA
Or non parliamo.
Ecco qui le due nozze:
riceverle dobbiam; alfin si tratta
d'una vostra protetta.
Seggiam.

IL CONTE
Seggiamo.

(tra sé)

E meditiam vendetta.

(Siedono.)

FIGARO

Why not?
I never dispute what I don't know.

(A Spanish march is heard in the distance.)

No. 22 Finale [41]

FIGARO

There's the march… let's go.
Take your places, ladies, take your places.
Susanna give me your arm.

SUSANNA

Here it is.

(Figaro takes Antonio with one arm and Susanna with the other; exeunt all except the Count and Countess.)

COUNT *(aside)*

Such presumption!

COUNTESS *(aside)*

I feel like ice.

COUNT

My lady…

COUNTESS

Say no more now.
Here are the two couples:
we must receive them;
one especially has your protection.
Let us sit down.

COUNT

Let's sit.

(aside)

And plan my revenge.

(They take their seats.)

Scena XIV

Entrano cacciatori con fucili in spalla; gente del foro; contadini e contadine; due giovinette che portano il cappello verginale con piume bianche; due altre un bianco velo; due altre i guanti e il mazzetto di fiori; due altre giovinette che portano un simile cappello per Susanna ecc.; Figaro con Marcellina; Bartolo con Susanna; Antonio, Barbarina ecc.; Bartolo conduce Susanna al Conte e s'inginocchia per ricever da lui il cappello ecc.; Figaro conduce Marcellina alla Contessa e fa la stessa funzione.

DUE CONTADINE

Amanti costanti, [42]
seguaci d'onor,
cantate, lodate
sì saggio signor.
A un dritto cedendo
che oltraggia, che offende,
ei caste vi rende
ai vostri amator.

TUTTI

Cantiamo, lodiamo
sì saggio signor!

(Susanna, essendo in ginocchio durante il duo, tira il Conte per l'abito, e gli mostra il bigliettino; dopo passa la mano – dal lato degli spettatori – alla testa, dove pare che il Conte le aggiusti il cappello, e gli dà il biglietto. Il Conte se lo mette furtivamente in seno. Susanna s'alza e gli fa una riverenza. Figaro viene a riceverla, e si balla il fandango. Marcellina s'alza un po' più tardi. Bartolo viene a riceverla dalle mani della Contessa. Il Conte va da un lato, cava il biglietto e fa l'atto d'un uom che rimase punto al dito; lo scuote, lo preme, lo succhia; e, vedendo il biglietto sigillato colla spilla, dice, gittando la spilla a terra e intanto che l'orchestra suona pianissimo:) [43]

Scene XIV

Enter hunters with rifles on their shoulders; lawyers; peasant men and women; two young girls carrying a bridal headdress with white feathers; two others, a white veil; two more, gloves and a bouquet of flowers; two more young girls carrying another bridal cap for Susanna and so on; Figaro with Marcellina; Bartolo with Susanna; Antonio, Barbarina and so on; Bartolo leads Susanna to the Count, and she kneels to receive the headdress etc. from him. Figaro leads Marcellina up to the Countess and does the same.

TWO PEASANT GIRLS
Faithful and [42]
honourable girls,
sing praises
to our wise lord.
By renouncing a right
which outraged and offended,
he leaves you pure
for your lovers.

ALL
Let us sing praises
to our wise lord.

(Susanna, while kneeling during the chorus, pulls the Count's coat, shows him the letter, then lifts her hand on the audience's side to her head, where the Count takes the letter under cover of adjusting her headdress. He puts it furtively in his breast pocket. Susanna rises, making him a curtsey; Figaro comes to receive her, and a fandango is danced. Marcellina rises slightly after; Bartolo comes to receive her from the Countess's hands. The Count moves aside, takes out the letter and pricks his finger; he shakes it, presses it, sucks it; seeing the letter sealed with a pin, he throws the pin down and says, as the orchestra plays very softly:) [43]

IL CONTE
Eh già, solita usanza:
le donne ficcan gli aghi in ogni loco.
Ah, ah, capisco il gioco.

FIGARO *(vede tutto e dice a Susanna)*
Un biglietto amoroso
che gli diè nel passar qualche galante,
ed era sigillato d'una spilla,
ond'ei si punse il dito,

(Il Conte legge, bacia il biglietto, cerca la spilla, la trova e se la mette alla manica del saio.)

Il Narciso or la cerca. Oh, che stordito!

Recitativo

IL CONTE
Andate, amici! E sia per questa sera
disposto l'apparato nuziale
colla più ricca pompa; io vo' che sia
magnifica la festa, e canti e fuochi,
e gran cena, e gran ballo, e ognuno impari
com'io tratto color, che a me son cari.

DUE CONTADINE
Amanti costanti,
seguaci d'onor,
cantate, lodate
sì saggio signor.
A un dritto cedendo
che oltraggia, che offende,
ei caste vi rende
ai vostri amator.

TUTTI
Cantiamo, lodiamo
sì saggio signor!

(Il coro e la marcia si ripetono e tutti partono.)

COUNT
Just like a woman,
to stick a pin in everywhere.
Ha, ha! I see her meaning.

FIGARO *(watching it all; to Susanna)*
Some flirt, in passing,
has slipped him a billet-doux
sealed with a pin,
on which he's pricked his finger.

(The Count reads the letter, kisses it, looks for the pin, finds it and puts it in his sleeve.)

Our Narcissus is looking for it. What a fool!

Recitative

COUNT
Now go, friends, and let the wedding
celebration be arranged for this evening
with the richest ceremony. I wish there
to be splendid entertainment, with singing
and fireworks, a grand banquet and ball;
you shall see how I treat those dear to me.

TWO PEASANT GIRLS
Faithful and
honourable girls,
sing praises
to our wise lord.
By renouncing a right
which outraged and offended,
he leaves you pure
for your lovers.

ALL
Let us sing praises
to our wise lord.

(The chorus and march are repeated: exeunt all.)

ATTO QUARTO

Scena I

Folto giardino con due padiglioni praticabili, l'uno a dritta e l'altro a sinistra. Notte. Barbarina sola.

N°23 Cavatina

BARBARINA *(cercando qualche cosa per terra)*
L'ho perduta… me meschina… [44]
ah, chi sa dove sarà?
Non la trovo… E mia cugina…
e il padron… cosa dirà?

Scena II

Entra Figaro con Marcellina.

Recitativo

FIGARO
Barbarina, cos'hai?

BARBARINA
L'ho perduta, cugino.

FIGARO
Cosa?

MARCELLINA
Cosa?

BARBARINA
La spilla,
che a me diede il padrone
per recar a Susanna.

FIGARO
A Susanna… la spilla?
E così, tenerella,

ACT FOUR

Scene I

A closely planted garden with two pavilions, their entrances to right and left. Night. Barbarina alone.

No. 23 Cavatina

BARBARINA *(searching for something on the ground)*
Oh dear me, I've lost it... [44]
Oh, wherever can it be?
I can't find it... my cousin
and my lord... what will they say?

Scene II

Enter Figaro and Marcellina.

Recitative

FIGARO
What's the matter, Barbarina?

BARBARINA
Oh cousin, I've lost it.

FIGARO
What?

MARCELLINA
What?

BARBARINA
The pin
his lordship gave me
to take back to Susanna.

FIGARO
To Susanna? The pin?
Even at your age

il mestiero già sai…
di far tutto sì ben quel che tu fai?

BARBARINA
Cos'è, vai meco in collera?

FIGARO
E non vedi ch'io scherzo? Osserva…

(cerca un momento per terra, dopo aver destramente cavata una spilla dall'abito o dalla cuffia di Marcellina, e la dà a Barbarina)

Questa
è la spilla che il Conte
da recare ti diede alla Susanna,
e servia di sigillo a un bigliettino;
vedi s'io sono istrutto.

BARBARINA
E perché il chiedi a me quando sai tutto?

FIGARO
Avea gusto d'udir come il padrone
ti diè la commissione.

BARBARINA
Che miracoli!
'Tieni, fanciulla, reca questa spilla
alla bella Susanna, e dille: "Questo
è il sigillo de' pini."'

FIGARO
Ah, ah, de' pini!

BARBARINA
È ver ch'ei mi soggiunse:
'Guarda che alcun non veda.'
Ma tu già tacerai.

FIGARO
Sicuramente.

you know the practices...
Do you do everything so well?

BARBARINA
Why are you getting angry with me?

FIGARO
Can't you see I'm joking? Look...

(searching the ground for a moment, after having dexterously taken a pin from Marcellina's dress or cap, and giving it to Barbarina)

This
is the pin the Count gave you
to take back to Susanna:
it was used to seal a note.
You see, I know all about it.

BARBARINA
Then why ask me if you know it all?

FIGARO
I wanted to hear how his lordship
sent you on this errand.

BARBARINA
Nothing remarkable!
'Here, my girl, take this pin
to pretty Susanna, and say: "This
is the seal of the pine grove."'

FIGARO
Aha! The pine grove!

BARBARINA
Oh yes, and then he added:
'Take care no one sees you!'
But you won't tell?

FIGARO
Trust me.

BARBARINA
A te già niente preme.

FIGARO
Oh niente, niente.

BARBARINA
Addio, mio bel cugino;
vo da Susanna, e poi da Cherubino.

(parte saltando)

Scena III

Marcellina e Figaro

FIGARO
Madre!

MARCELLINA
Figlio!

FIGARO
Son morto!

MARCELLINA
Calmati, figlio mio.

FIGARO
Son morto, dico.

MARCELLINA
Flemma, flemma, e poi flemma! Il fatto è serio;
e pensarci convien, ma pensa un poco
che ancor non sai di chi si prenda gioco.

FIGARO
Ah, quella spilla, oh madre, è quella stessa
che poc'anzi ei raccolse.

MARCELLINA
È ver, ma questo
al più ti porge un dritto

BARBARINA
It can't concern you at all.

FIGARO
Oh, not at all.

BARBARINA
Well, goodbye, cousin:
I'm going to Susanna and then to Cherubino.

(she dances off)

Scene III

Marcellina and Figaro

FIGARO
Mother...

MARCELLINA
My son?

FIGARO
All is over.

MARCELLINA
Calm yourself, my son.

FIGARO
All is over, I say.

MARCELLINA
Patience, patience and yet more patience;
things are serious, and we must think them out.
But wait, you don't know whom the joke is on.

FIGARO
Oh mother, that pin was the one
he picked up a little while ago.

MARCELLINA
That's true... but this only
gives you the opportunity

di stare in guardia e vivere in sospetto.
Ma non sai, se in effetto...

FIGARO
All'erta dunque: il loco del congresso
so dov'è stabilito...

MARCELLINA
Dove vai figlio mio?

FIGARO
A vendicar tutti i mariti: addio.

(parte infuriato)

Scena IV

Marcellina sola.

MARCELLINA
Presto avvertiam Susanna:
io la credo innocente: quella faccia,
quell'aria di modestia... È caso ancora
ch'ella non fosse... ah quando il cor non ciurma
personale interesse,
ogni donna è portata alla difesa
del suo povero sesso,
da questi uomini ingrati a torto oppresso.

N°24 *Aria*

Il capro e la capretta [45]
son sempre in amistà,
l'agnello all'agnelletta
la guerra mai non fa.
Le più feroci belve
per selve e per campagne
lascian le lor compagne
in pace e libertà.

to be on your guard and keep your eyes open.
But you don't know if in fact...

FIGARO
I'll be on the alert! I know
where the meeting has been arranged for.

MARCELLINA
Where are you going, my son?

FIGARO
To avenge all husbands. Farewell.

(exit furiously)

Scene IV

Marcellina alone.

MARCELLINA
Quickly, I must warn Susanna:
I believe her innocent: that face...
that air of modesty... And yet even
were she not... Ah! when her heart
is not personally involved,
every woman is drawn to the defence
of her own poor sex,
so unjustly oppressed by these ungrateful men.

N°24 Aria

The billy goat and she-goat [45]
always remain friends,
the sheep and ewe
never make war.
The fiercest beasts
in the forests and the wilds
leave their companions
in peace and liberty.

Sol noi povere femmine, [46]
che tanto amiam questi uomini,
trattate siam dai perfidi
ognor con crudeltà!

(parte)

Scena V

Barbarina sola con alcune frutta e ciambelle.

Recitativo

BARBARINA
'Nel padiglione a manca' – ei così disse.
È questo, è questo... E poi, se non venisse?
Oh ve' che brava gente! A stento darmi
un arancio, una pera e una ciambella.
'Per chi madamigella?'
'Oh, per qualcun, signore.'
'Già lo sappiam.' Ebbene,
il padron l'odia, ed io gli voglio bene;
però costommi un bacio, e cosa importa,
forse qualcun me'l renderà.

(sente arrivare qualcuno)

Son morta!

(Fugge, ed entra nel padiglione a sinistra.)

Scena VI

Figaro; poi Bartolo, Basilio e lavoratori.

FIGARO *(solo con mantello e lanternino)*
È Barbarina...

(ode venir gente)

Chi va là?

But we, poor women, [46]
who love these men so much,
are always treated with cruelty
by the perfidious creatures!

(exit)

Scene V

Barbarina alone, with some fruit and sweetmeats.

Recitative

BARBARINA
'In the left-hand pavilion,' he said.
This is it… this is it. Suppose he doesn't come?
Oh, these tiresome people! I could hardly get them
to give me an apple, a pear and a pastry.
'Who's it for, my dear?'
'It's for someone, sir.'
'We know that.' Oh well,
his lordship hates him, but I love him;
it cost me a kiss, but what does it matter?
Someone's bound to pay it back.

(hearing someone coming)

Mercy on us!

(She flees in fright into the left pavilion.)

Scene VI

Figaro; then Bartolo, Basilio and workers.

FIGARO *(alone with a cloak and dark lantern)*
That's Barbarina.

(hearing people approaching)

Who goes there?

BASILIO *(entra con Bartolo e truppa di lavoratori)*
Son quelli
che invitasti a venir.

BARTOLO
Che brutto ceffo!
Sembri un cospirator. Che diamin sono
quegli infausti apparati?

FIGARO
Lo vedrete tra poco.
In questo stesso loco
celebrerem la festa
della mia sposa onesta
e del feudal signor…

BASILIO
Ah, buono, buono!
Capisco come egli è,

(tra sé)

Accordati si son senza di me.

FIGARO
Voi da questi contorni
non vi scostate; intanto
io vado a dar certi ordini,
e torno in pochi istanti.
A un fischio mio correte tutti quanti.

(Partono tutti, eccettuati Bartolo e Basilio.)

Scena VII

Basilio e Bartolo.

BASILIO
Ha i diavoli nel corpo.

BARTOLO
Ma cosa, quanti?

BASILIO *(entering with Bartolo and a group of workmen)*
Those whom
you invited to come.

BARTOLO
What a sinister scowl!
You look like a conspirator;
what on earth is all this mystery about?

FIGARO
You'll soon see.
In this very spot
there'll be celebrated the union
of my virtuous bride
and our feudal lord...

BASILIO
Ah, good, good!
I see now how it is.

(aside)

They've settled it without me.

FIGARO
Do not go away
from hereabouts: meanwhile
I must go and give some instructions;
I'll be back very shortly;
when I whistle, all of you rush out.

(Exeunt all, except Bartolo and Basilio.)

Scene VII

Basilio and Bartolo.

BASILIO
He's possessed by demons.

BARTOLO
But what is going on?

BASILIO

Nulla.
Susanna piace al Conte; ella d'accordo
gli diè un appuntamento
che a Figaro non piace.

BARTOLO
E che, dunque dovria soffrirlo in pace?

BASILIO
Quel che soffrono tanti
ei soffrir non potrebbe? E poi sentite,
che guadagno può far? Nel mondo, amico,
l'accozzarla co' grandi
fu pericolo ognora:
dan novanta per cento, e han vinto ancora.

N°25 Aria

BASILIO
In quegli anni in cui val poco [47]
la mal pratica ragion,
ebbi anch'io lo stesso foco,
fui quel pazzo ch'or non son.
Ma col tempo e coi perigli
Donna Flemma capitò;
e i capricci, ed i puntigli
dalla testa mi cavò.
Presso un picciolo abituro
seco lei mi trasse un giorno,
e togliendo giù dal muro
del pacifico soggiorno
una pelle di somaro,
'Prendi,' disse, 'o figlio caro.'
Poi disparve, e mi lasciò.
Mentre ancor tacito [48]
guardo quel dono,
il ciel s'annuvola
rimbomba il tuono,
mista alla grandine
scroscia la piova:

BASILIO

Nothing.

Susanna pleases the Count.
She has agreed to give him a rendezvous,
and that doesn't please Figaro.

BARTOLO

So what? He'll have to grin and bear it.

BASILIO

Couldn't he bear
what so many do? And then, listen:
what can he gain? In this world, my friend,
it is always dangerous
to get mixed up with the masters:
they give you ninety per cent and always emerge the winners.

No. 25 Aria

BASILIO

In those years when reason [47]
little practised, carried little weight,
I too had that same fire,
and was the kind of fool I no longer am.
But with time and dangers
Dame Discretion appeared,
and drove whims and scruples
out of my head.
Near a little hut
she led me one day with her and,
taking down from the wall
of the peaceful dwelling
an ass's skin,
said, 'Take this, my dear son!'
Then she vanished and left me.
While I was still mutely [48]
looking at her gift,
the sky grew cloudy
and there was a roll of thunder;
rain and hail
came pouring down;

ecco le membra
coprir mi giova
col manto d'asino
che mi donò.
Finisce il turbine,
né fo due passi
che fiera orribile
dianzi a me fassi;
già già mi tocca
l'ingorda bocca,
già di difendermi
speme non ho.
Ma il fiuto ignobile
del mio vestito
tolse alla belva
sì l'appetito
che disprezzandomi
si rinselvò.
Così conoscere
mi fè la sorte,
ch'onte, pericoli,
vergogna e morte
col cuoio d'asino
fuggir si può.

(Basilio e Bartolo partono.)

Scena VIII

Figaro solo.

N°26 *Recitativo ed Aria*

FIGARO
Tutto è disposto: l'ora
dovrebbe esser vicina; io sento gente…
È dessa… non è alcun… buia è la notte…
ed io comincio omai
a fare il scimunito
mestiere di marito…
Ingrata! Nel momento

to cover myself
I was glad
of the ass's skin
she had given me.
When the whirling storm had passed,
I took two steps
to find a fearsome beast
before me;
already his greedy maw
was touching me,
and I could not hope
to defend myself.
But the loathsome smell
of my cloak
so took away
the beast's appetite
that, disdaining me,
he returned to the forest.
So fate
taught me,
that insults, dangers,
shame and death
can be escaped
under an ass's skin.

(Exeunt Basilio and Bartolo.)

Scena VIII

Figaro alone.

No. 26 Recitative and Aria

FIGARO
Everything is ready; the hour
must be at hand; I heard someone…
Is it she?… no, no one… it's very dark
tonight… and now I begin
to learn the foolish art
of being a husband.
Traitress! at the very moment

della mia cerimonia…
ei godeva leggendo, e nel vederlo
io rideva di me, senza saperlo.
Oh Susanna, Susanna,
quanta pena mi costi!
Con quell'ingenua faccia,
con quegli occhi innocenti…
Chi creduto l'avria!…
Ah, che il fidarsi a donna è ognor follia.

Aprite un po' quegli occhi, [49]
uomini incauti e sciocchi,
guardate queste femmine,
guardate cosa son!
Queste chiamate dèe
dagli ingannati sensi,
a cui tributa incensi
la debole ragion,
son streghe che incantano
per farci penar,
sirene che cantano
per farci affogar,
civette che allettano
per trarci le piume,
comete che brillano
per toglierci il lume;
son rose spinose,
son volpi vezzose,
son orse benigne,
colombe maligne,
maestre d'inganni,
amiche d'affanni
che fingono, mentono,
amore non senton,
non senton pietà,
no, no, no, no!
Il resto nol dico,
già ognuno lo sa!

(Si ritira.)

of our wedding…
he reading with pleasure, and I,
watching him, unwittingly laughing at myself.
Oh Susanna, Susanna,
what anguish you have cost me!
With that sweet face
and those innocent eyes…
Who would have believed it!…
Ah, to trust women is sheer folly.

Just open your eyes, [49]
you rash and foolish men,
and look at these women:
see them as they are,
these goddesses, so called
by the intoxicated senses,
to whom feeble reason
offers tribute.
They are witches who cast spells
for our torment,
sirens who sing
for our confusion,
coquettes who fascinate
to pluck us,
comets who dazzle
to deprive us of light;
they are thorned roses,
alluring vixens,
smiling she-bears,
malign doves,
masters of deceit,
friends of distress
who cheat and lie,
who feel no love
and have no pity,
no, no, no, no!
The rest I need not say,
for everyone knows it already.

(He withdraws.)

Scena IX

La Contessa, Susanna, Marcellina, e Figaro in disparte.

Entrano la Contessa e Susanna, ciascuna travestita con gli abiti dell'altra, e Marcellina.

Recitativo

SUSANNA
Signora, ella mi disse
che Figaro verravvi.

MARCELLINA
Anzi è venuto.
Abbassa un po' la voce.

SUSANNA
Dunque, un ci ascolta, e l'altro
dée venir a cercarmi,
incominciam.

MARCELLINA
Io voglio qui celarmi.

(Entra dove entrò Barbarina.)

Scena X

La Contessa, Susanna e Figaro.

SUSANNA
Madama, voi tremate; avreste freddo?

LA CONTESSA
Parmi umida la notte; io mi ritiro.

FIGARO *(tra sé)*
Eccoci della crisi al grande istante.

Scene IX

The Countess, Susanna, Marcellina; Figaro apart.

Enter the Countess and Susanna dressed in each other's clothes, and Marcellina.

Recitative

SUSANNA
Marcellina told me, my lady,
that Figaro would be coming.

MARCELLINA
He's here already.
Lower your voice a little.

SUSANNA
So one's listening, the other
should be coming to find me.
We can begin.

MARCELLINA
I'll hide myself in here.

(She goes into the same place as Barbarina.)

Scene X

The Countess, Susanna and Figaro.

SUSANNA
Madam, you are trembling; are you cold?

COUNTESS
The night is rather chilly… I'll go in.

FIGARO *(aside)*
Now comes the climax of the drama.

SUSANNA
Io sotto questi piante,
se madama il permette,
resto a prendere il fresco una mezz'ora.

FIGARO *(tra sé)*
Il fresco, il fresco!

LA CONTESSA *(si nasconde)*
Restaci in buon'ora.

SUSANNA *(tra sé)*
Il birbo è in sentinella.
Divertiamci anche noi,
diamogli la mercè de' dubbi suoi.

N°27 Recitativo ed Aria

SUSANNA
Giunse alfin il momento
che godrò senz'affanno
in braccio all'idol mio. Timide cure,
uscite dal mio petto,
a turbar non venite il mio diletto!
Oh, come par che all'amoroso foco
l'amenità del loco,
la terra e il ciel risponda,
come la notte i furti miei seconda!

Deh vieni, non tardar, oh gioia bella, [50]
vieni ove amore per goder t'appella,
finché non splende in ciel notturna face,
finché l'aria è ancor bruna e il mondo tace.
Qui mormora il ruscel, qui scherza l'aura,
che col dolce sussurro il cor ristaura,
qui ridono i fioretti e l'erba è fresca,
ai piaceri d'amor qui tutto adesca.
Vieni, ben mio, tra queste piante ascose,
ti vo' la fronte incoronar di rose.

SUSANNA

If your ladyship will allow me,
I'll stay among the pine trees
to take the air for half an hour.

FIGARO *(aside)*

To take the air!

COUNTESS *(she hides herself)*

Stay, and take your time.

SUSANNA *(aside)*

The rascal's watching,
so we'll have some fun.
We'll reward him for his doubts,

No. 27 Recitative and Aria

SUSANNA

At last comes the moment
when, without reserve, I can rejoice
in my lover's arms: timid scruples,
hence from my heart,
and do not come to trouble my delight.
Oh, how the spirit of this place,
the earth and the sky, seem
to echo the fire of love!
How the night furthers my stealth!

Come, do not delay, oh bliss, [50]
come where love calls thee to joy,
while night's torch does not shine in the sky,
while the air is still dark and the world quiet.
Here murmurs the stream, here sports the breeze,
which refreshes the heart with its sweet whispers.
Here flowers smile and the grass is cool;
here everything invites to the pleasures of love.
Come, my dearest, and amid these sheltered trees
I will wreathe thy brow with roses.

[1789 version]

N°27a Rondò

SUSANNA
Al desio di chi t'adora [51]
vieni, vola, o mia speranza!
Morirò, se indarno ancora
tu mi lasci sospirar.
Le promesse, i giuramenti,
deh! rammenta, o mio tesoro!
e i momenti di ristoro
che mi fece Amor sperar!
Ah! ch'io mai più non resisto
all'ardor che in sen m'accende!
Chi d'amor gli affetti intende,
compatisca il mio penar.

Scena XI

La Contessa, Susanna, Figaro e Cherubino; poi il Conte.

Recitativo

FIGARO *(tra sé)*
Perfida, e in quella forma
ella meco mentia? Non so s'io vegli o dorma.

CHERUBINO *(entra canterellando)*
La la la, la la la la...

LA CONTESSA *(tra sé)*
Il picciol paggio!

CHERUBINO
Io sento gente, entriamo
ove entrò Barbarina.

(scorgendo la Contessa)

Oh, vedo qui una donna.

[1789 version]

No. 27a Rondò

SUSANNA
To the desire of one who adores you, [51]
come, hasten, my darling!
I shall die if you let me
sigh longer in vain.
My treasure, I beg you, remember
your promises, your vows,
and those moments of solace
which Love has made me hope for!
Ah, I can no longer resist
the passion burning in my breast!
May those who feel the pangs of love
take pity on my suffering.

Scene XI

The Countess, Susanna, Figaro and Cherubino; then the Count.

Recitative

FIGARO *(aside)*
The traitress! this is how
she was deceiving me. I don't know if I am awake or dreaming.

CHERUBINO *(entering singing)*
La la la, la la la la...

COUNTESS *(aside)*
The page!

CHERUBINO
I hear someone: I'll go
where I can find Barbarina.

(discovering the Countess)

Ah, I see a woman!

LA CONTESSA *(tra sé)*

Ahi, me meschina!

CHERUBINO

M'inganno! A quel cappello
che nell'ombra vegg'io parmi Susanna.

LA CONTESSA

E se il Conte ora vien? Sorte tiranna!

N°28 Finale

CHERUBINO *(tra sé)*

Pian pianin le andrò più presso, [52]
tempo perso non sarà.

LA CONTESSA *(tra sé)*

Ah, se il Conte arriva adesso
qualche imbroglio accaderà!

CHERUBINO *(alla Contessa)*

Susannetta…

(tra sé)

non risponde…
colla mano il volto asconde…
or la burlo, in verità.

(La prende per la mano, l'accarezza; la Contessa cerca di liberarsi.)

LA CONTESSA *(alterando la voce a tempo)*

Arditello, sfacciatello,
ite presto via di qua!

CHERUBINO

Smorfiosa, maliziosa,
io già so perché sei qua!

IL CONTE *(da lontano, in atteggiamento d'uno che guarda)*

Ecco qui la mia Susanna!

COUNTESS *(aside)*

Woe is me!

CHERUBINO

Surely not! By that hat I thought
I recognized Susanna in the darkness.

COUNTESS

If the Count should come now! Cruel fate!

No. 28 Finale

CHERUBINO *(aside)*

Very softly I'll approach her; [52]
my time will not be wasted.

COUNTESS *(aside)*

Oh, if the Count should arrive now,
what confusion there will be!

CHERUBINO *(to the Countess)*

Dear Susanna…

(aside)

she doesn't answer…
she hides her face with her hand…
now I'll really tease her.

(He takes her hand and caresses it; the Countess tries to free herself.)

COUNTESS *(disguising her voice)*

Impudent fellow,
be off from here at once.

CHERUBINO

Affected flirt,
I know why you're here.

COUNT *(peering at them from a distance)*

There is my Susanna!

SUSANNA e FIGARO *(lontani l'uno dall'altro)*
Ecco qui l'uccellatore.

CHERUBINO *(alla Contessa)*
Non far meco la tiranna.

SUSANNA, IL CONTE e FIGARO *(tra sé)*
Ah, nel sen mi batte il core!
Un altr'uom con lei si sta.

LA CONTESSA *(sottovoce a Cherubino)*
Via partite, o chiamo gente!

CHERUBINO *(sempre tenendola per la mano)*
Dammi un bacio, o non fai niente.

SUSANNA, IL CONTE e FIGARO *(tra sé)*
Alla voce, è quegli il paggio.

LA CONTESSA *(come sopra)*
Anche un bacio, che coraggio!

CHERUBINO
E perché far io non posso,
quel che il Conte ognor farà?

SUSANNA, LA CONTESSA, IL CONTE e FIGARO *(tra sé)*
Temerario!

CHERUBINO
Oh ve', che smorfie!
Sai ch'io fui dietro il sofà.

SUSANNA, LA CONTESSA, IL CONTE e FIGARO *(tra sé)*
Se il ribaldo ancor sta saldo
la faccenda guasterà.

CHERUBINO
Prendi intanto…

(Il paggio vuol dare un bacio alla Contessa; il Conte si mette in mezzo e riceve il bacio egli stesso.)

SUSANNA and FIGARO *(distant one from the other)*
Here's the bird-catcher.

CHERUBINO *(to the Countess)*
Don't be so hard on me!

SUSANNA, COUNT and FIGARO *(aside)*
How my heart beats in my breast!
Another man is there with her.

COUNTESS *(softly, to Cherubino)*
Go away, or I'll call for help.

CHERUBINO *(still holding her hand)*
Give me a kiss, or you'll do nothing.

SUSANNA, COUNT and FIGARO *(aside)*
By his voice, that's the page.

COUNTESS *(as above)*
What, a kiss? What insolence!

CHERUBINO
And why can't I do
what the Count's about to do?

SUSANNA, COUNTESS, COUNT and FIGARO *(aside)*
What effrontery!

CHERUBINO
Don't be so prudish!
You know I was behind the sofa.

SUSANNA, COUNTESS, COUNT and FIGARO *(aside)*
If the wretch persists in being obstinate,
he will ruin all our plan.

CHERUBINO
Take a kiss then...

(He tries to kiss the Countess, but the Count intervenes and receives the kiss himself.)

LA CONTESSA e CHERUBINO
Oh cielo, il Conte!

(Il paggio entra da Barbarina.)

FIGARO *(tra sé)*
Vo' veder cosa fan là.

IL CONTE
Perché voi nol ripetete,
ricevete questo qua!

(Il Conte vuol dare uno schiaffo a Cherubino; Figaro in questo s'appressa e lo riceve egli stesso; Susanna, che ode lo schiaffo, ride.)

FIGARO *(tra sé)*
Ah, ci ho fatto un bel guadagno
colla mia curiosità!

LA CONTESSA e IL CONTE
Ah, ci ha fatto un bel guadagno
colla sua temerità!

SUSANNA
Ah, ci ha fatto un bel guadagno
colla sua curiosità!

(Figaro si ritira.)

COUNT *(alla Contessa)*
Partito è alfin l'audace,
accostati ben mio!

LA CONTESSA
Giacché così vi piace,
eccomi qui signor.

FIGARO
Che compiacente femmina!
Che sposa di buon cor!

IL CONTE
Porgimi la manina!

COUNTESS and CHERUBINO
Oh Heavens! The Count!

(The page joins Barbarina.)

FIGARO *(aside)*
I must see what's going on there.

COUNT
Since you won't behave,
take that, then.

(He goes to slap Cherubino, but Figaro approaches at this moment and receives it himself. Susanna, who has seen the slap, laughs.)

FIGARO *(aside)*
Ah! That's the reward
my curiosity has brought me.

COUNTESS and COUNT
Ah! That's the reward
his temerity has brought him.

SUSANNA
Ah! That's the reward
his curiosity has brought him.

(Figaro retires.)

COUNT *(to the Countess)*
At last that impudent fellow's gone;
come nearer, my dear,

COUNTESS
As you wish.
Here I am, my lord.

FIGARO
What an obliging girl!
What an open-hearted bride!

COUNT
Give me your little hand.

LA CONTESSA
Io ve la do.

IL CONTE
Carina!

FIGARO
Carina!

IL CONTE
Che dita tenerelle!
Che delicata pelle!
Mi pizzica, mi stuzzica,
m'empie d'un nuovo ardor.

SUSANNA, LA CONTESSA e FIGARO
La cieca prevenzione
delude la ragione,
inganna i sensi ognor.

IL CONTE
Oltre la dote, o cara,
ricevi anco un brillante,
che a te porge un amante
in pegno del suo amor.

(Le dà un anello.)

LA CONTESSA
Tutto Susanna piglia
dal suo benefattor.

SUSANNA, IL CONTE e FIGARO *(tra sé)*
Va tutto a maraviglia,
ma il meglio manca ancor.

LA CONTESSA *(al Conte)*
Signor, d'accese fiaccole
io veggio il balenar.

COUNTESS
Here it is.

COUNT
My dearest!

FIGARO
His dearest?

COUNT
What slender fingers,
what delicate skin!
They pierce me through and through
and fill me with new ardour.

SUSANNA, COUNTESS and FIGARO
His blind infatuation
deludes his reason
and deceives all his senses.

COUNT
Besides your dowry, my dearest,
take this jewel too,
which a lover gives you
as token of his love.

(He gives her a ring.)

COUNTESS
Susanna owes everything
to her benefactor.

SUSANNA, COUNT and FIGARO *(aside)*
Everything is going splendidly!
But the best is yet to come.

COUNTESS *(to the Count)*
My lord, I see the glow
of kindled torches.

IL CONTE
Entriam, mia bella Venere,
andiamoci a celar!

SUSANNA e FIGARO *(tra sé)*
Mariti scimuniti,
venite ad imparar!

LA CONTESSA
Al buio, signor mio?

IL CONTE
È quello che vogl'io.
Tu sai che là per leggere
io non desio d'entrar.

FIGARO *(tra sé)*
La perfida lo séguita,
è vano il dubitar.

SUSANNA e LA CONTESSA *(tra sé)*
I furbi sono in trappola,
comincia ben l'affar.

(Figaro passa.)

IL CONTE *(con voce alterata)*
Chi passa?

FIGARO *(con rabbia)*
Passa gente!

LA CONTESSA *(sottovoce al Conte)*
È Figaro; men vo!

IL CONTE
Andate; io poi verrò.

(Il Conte si disperde nel folto, la Contessa entra nel padiglione a destra.)

COUNT
Come then, my Venus,
let us conceal ourselves in here.

SUSANNA and FIGARO *(aside)*
Foolish husbands,
come and learn your lesson.

COUNTESS
In the dark, my lord?

COUNT
That's what I would have:
you know I'm not going there
in order to read.

FIGARO *(aside)*
Now she's followed him,
I cannot doubt her deceit.

SUSANNA and COUNTESS *(aside)*
The rogues are in the trap;
the play is going well.

(Figaro passes.)

COUNT *(disguising his voice)*
Who's there?

FIGARO *(enraged)*
What's it to you?

COUNTESS *(softly, to the Count)*
That's Figaro; I'm going.

COUNT
Go on: I'll rejoin you soon.

(The Count retires among the trees, while the Countess goes into the pavilion on the right).

FIGARO
Tutto è tranquillo e placido: [53]
entrò la bella Venere;
col vago Marte a prendere
nuovo Vulcan del secolo
in rete la potrò.

SUSANNA *(con voce alterata)*
Ehi, Figaro, tacete! [54]

FIGARO
Oh, questa è la Contessa...

(a Susanna)

A tempo qui giungete...
Vedrete là voi stessa...
il Conte e la mia sposa...
di propria man la cosa
toccar io vi farò.

SUSANNA *(si dimentica di alterar la voce)*
Parlate un po' più basso,
di qua non muovo il passo,
ma vendicar mi vò.

FIGARO *(tra sé)*
Susanna!

(a Susanna)

Vendicarsi?

SUSANNA
Sì.

FIGARO
Come potria farsi?

SUSANNA *(tra sé)*
L'iniquo io vo' sorprendere,
poi so quel che farò.

FIGARO
All is quiet and peaceful: [53]
fair Venus has gone in;
to take her with her lover Mars,
like a modern Vulcan
I'll catch them in my net.

SUSANNA *(disguising her voice)*
Hey, Figaro! Keep quiet! [54]

FIGARO
Ah, that is the Countess...

(to Susanna)

You came in time.
There you'll see for yourself
the Count and my bride;
you can touch them
with your own hand.

SUSANNA *(forgetting to change her voice)*
Speak a little softer:
I shall not stir from here,
but I will be avenged.

FIGARO *(aside)*
Susanna!

(to Susanna)

Be avenged?

SUSANNA
Yes.

FIGARO
How can you do this?

SUSANNA *(aside)*
I'll trap the villain,
then I'll know what to do.

FIGARO *(tra sé)*
La volpe vuol sorprendermi,
e secondarla vò.

SUSANNA *(tra sé)*
L'iniquo io vo' sorprendere;
poi so quel che farò.

FIGARO
Ah, se madama il vuole!

SUSANNA
Su via, manco parole.

FIGARO *(come sopra)*
Eccomi a' vostri piedi…
ho pieno il cor di foco.
Esaminate il loco…
pensate al traditor.

SUSANNA *(tra sé)*
Come la man mi pizzica!
Che smania, che furor!

FIGARO *(tra sé)*
Come il polmon mi s'altera!
Che smania, che calor!

SUSANNA *(alterando la voce un poco)*
E senz'alcun affetto?

FIGARO
Suppliscavi il dispetto.
Non perdiam tempo invano,
datemi un po' la mano…

SUSANNA *(gli dà uno schiaffo parlando in voce naturale)*
Servitevi, signor!

FIGARO
Che schiaffo!

FIGARO *(aside)*
The vixen wants to trap me,
I'll lead her on.

SUSANNA *(aside)*
I'll trap the villain;
then I know what to do.

FIGARO
Ah, if my lady wishes it!

SUSANNA
Go on, don't waste words.

FIGARO *(as above)*
Here I kneel at your feet…
my heart full of fire.
Look at this spot…
and think how you were betrayed.

SUSANNA *(aside)*
How my hand tingles
with impatience and fury!

FIGARO *(aside)*
How my bosom heaves
with impatience and fire!

SUSANNA *(altering her voice a little)*
Without any love?

FIGARO
Let my indignation be sufficient.
Let's waste no more time in vain;
give me your hand…

SUSANNA *(speaking in her own voice, and slapping his face)*
Take that, sir!

FIGARO
What a blow!

SUSANNA *(lo schiaffeggia a tempo)*
E questo, e questo,
e ancora questo, e questo, e poi quest'altro!

FIGARO
Non batter così presto.

SUSANNA *(sempre schiaffeggiandolo)*
E questo, signor scaltro,
e questo, e poi quest'altro ancor.

FIGARO
Oh schiaffi graziosissimi!
Oh mio felice amor!

SUSANNA
Impara, impara, o perfido,
a fare il seduttor.

FIGARO *(si mette in ginocchio)*
Pace, pace, mio dolce tesoro, [55]
io conobbi la voce che adoro
e che impressa ognor serbo nel cor.

SUSANNA *(ridendo e con sorpresa)*
La mia voce?

FIGARO
La voce che adoro.

SUSANNA e FIGARO
Pace, pace, mio dolce tesoro,
pace, pace, mio tenero amor.

IL CONTE *(ritornando)*
Non la trovo e girai tutto il bosco.

SUSANNA e FIGARO
Questi è il Conte, alla voce il conosco.

IL CONTE *(verso il padiglione in cui è entrata la Contessa)*
Ehi, Susanna.. sei sorda… sei muta?

SUSANNA *(slapping him in time)*
And that too, and that,
and that, and that, and that as well!

FIGARO
Don't beat me so fast.

SUSANNA *(still slapping his face)*
And that, you rascal,
and that again.

FIGARO
How sweet these blows!
How happy is my love!

SUSANNA
That'll teach you, false one,
to play the seducer.

FIGARO *(kneeling)*
Now peace, my dearest treasure: [55]
I recognized the voice I love
and which keeps my heart in thrall.

SUSANNA *(laughing, in surprise)*
My voice?

FIGARO
The voice I adore.

SUSANNA and FIGARO
Then peace, my dearest treasure,
peace, my sweetest love.

COUNT *(re-entering)*
I can't find her, though I've been through all the wood.

FIGARO and SUSANNA
That's the Count, I recognize his voice.

COUNT *(towards the recess into which the Countess went)*
Susanna... are you deaf... are you dumb?

SUSANNA *(sottovoce a Figaro)*
Bella, bella! Non l'ha conosciuta.

FIGARO *(sottovoce a Susanna)*
Chi?

SUSANNA *(come sopra)*
Madama.

FIGARO *(come sopra)*
Madama?

SUSANNA *(come sopra)*
Madama!

SUSANNA e FIGARO *(sottovoce)*
La commedia, idol mio, terminiamo:
consoliamo il bizzarro amator!

FIGARO *(si mette ai piedi di Susanna)*
Sì, madama, voi siete il ben mio!

IL CONTE *(tra sé)*
La mia sposa! Ah, senz'arme son io!

FIGARO *(sempre inginocchiato)*
Un ristoro al mio cor concedete.

SUSANNA *(alterando la voce)*
Io son qui, faccio quel che volete.

IL CONTE *(tra sé)*
Ah, ribaldi!

SUSANNA e FIGARO
Ah, corriamo, mio bene,
e le pene compensi il piacer.

(Figaro s'alza, e i due vanno verso il padiglione a sinistra.)

SUSANNA *(softly, to Figaro)*
Oh lovely! He didn't recognize her!

FIGARO *(softly, to Susanna)*
Who?

SUSANNA *(as above)*
My lady.

FIGARO *(as above)*
My lady?

SUSANNA *(as above)*
My lady!

SUSANNA and FIGARO *(softly)*
Let's end this comedy, my dearest,
and console this strange lover.

FIGARO *(at Susanna's feet)*
Yes, my lady, you are my love.

COUNT *(aside)*
My wife! And I am unarmed!

FIGARO *(still kneeling)*
Grant some solace to my heart.

SUSANNA *(disguising her voice)*
Here I am: do what you will.

COUNT *(aside)*
How dare they!

SUSANNA and FIGARO
Let us hasten, love,
and let pleasure make up for our pain.

(Figaro rises, and they go towards the pavilion on the left.)

Scena XII

Il Conte, la Contessa, Susanna, Figaro, Marcellina, Bartolo, Cherubino, Barbarina, Antonio, Basilio, Don Curzio e servitori.

IL CONTE *(arresta Figaro)*
Gente, gente, all'armi, all'armi! [56]

(Susanna entra nel padiglione.)

FIGARO *(finge eccessiva paura)*
Il padrone! Son perduto!

IL CONTE
Gente, gente, aiuto, aiuto!

(Accorrono Antonio, Basilio, Bartolo, Don Curzio e servitori con fiaccole accese.)

BASILIO, DON CURZIO, ANTONIO e BARTOLO
Cosa avvenne?

IL CONTE
Il scellerato
m'ha tradito, m'ha infamato,
e con chi state a veder!

BASILIO, DON CURZIO, ANTONIO e BARTOLO *(tra sé)*
Son stordito, sbalordito,
non mi par che ciò sia ver!

FIGARO *(tra sé)*
Son storditi, sbalorditi,
oh che scena, che piacer!

IL CONTE
Invan resistete,
uscite, madama,
il premio or avrete
di vostra onestà!
Il paggio!

Scene XII

The Count, the Countess, Susanna, Figaro, Marcellina, Bartolo, Cherubino, Barbarina, Antonio, Basilio, Don Curzio, servants.

COUNT *(stopping Figaro)*
Ho there! Bring your swords! [56]

(Susanna goes into the pavilion.)

FIGARO *(pretending to be terrified)*
The master! I'm lost!

COUNT
Ho there, I say! Help!

(Antonio, Basilio, Bartolo, Don Curzio and servants with lighted torches run in.)

BASILIO, DON CURZIO, ANTONIO and BARTOLO
What's amiss?

COUNT
This scoundrel
has betrayed me, has shamed me,
and with whom, you shall see.

BASILIO, DON CURZIO, ANTONIO and BARTOLO *(aside)*
I'm astounded, I'm bewildered,
I can't believe it's true.

FIGARO *(aside)*
They're astounded, they're bewildered.
What a scene! oh what joy!

COUNT
In vain you resist:
come forth, my lady,
and receive the reward
or your virtue.
The page!

(Il Conte tira pel braccio Cherubino, che fa forza per non uscire, né si vede che per metà; dopo il paggio, escono Barbarina, Marcellina e Susanna, vestita cogli abiti della Contessa: si tiene il fazzoletto sulla faccia e s'inginocchia ai piedi del Conte.)

ANTONIO
Mia figlia!

FIGARO
Mia madre!

BASILIO, DON CURZIO, ANTONIO, BARTOLO e FIGARO
Madama!

IL CONTE
Scoperta è la trama,
la perfida è qua.

(S'inginocchiano tutti ad uno ad uno.)

SUSANNA
Perdono! Perdono!

IL CONTE
No, no, non sperarlo.

FIGARO
Perdono! Perdono!

IL CONTE
No, no, non vo' darlo!.

TUTTI tranne IL CONTE
Perdono! Perdono!

IL CONTE
No, no, no, no, no!

LA CONTESSA *(uscendo dall'altro padiglione)*
Almeno io per loro
perdono otterrò.

(The Count pulls out Cherubino by the arm, who attempts to resist and is only half seen; then follow Barbarina, Marcellina and Susanna, who, dressed in the Countess's clothes and holding a handkerchief to her face, kneels at the Count's feet.)

ANTONIO
My daughter!

FIGARO
My mother!

BASILIO, DON CURZIO, ANTONIO, BARTOLO and FIGARO
My lady!

COUNT
The plot is discovered,
the traitress is here.

(All kneel one after the other.)

SUSANNA
Forgive me, forgive me.

COUNT
No, no, do not hope for it.

FIGARO
Forgive me, forgive me.

COUNT
No, no I will not.

ALL except COUNT
Forgive us, forgive us.

COUNT
No, no, no, no, no!

COUNTESS *(coming out of the other pavilion)*
At least let me plead
forgiveness for them.

(Vuole inginocchiarsi; il Conte non lo permette.)

IL CONTE, BASILIO, DON CURZIO, ANTONIO e BARTOLO
Oh cielo, che veggio!
Deliro! Vaneggio!
Ché creder non so.

IL CONTE *(in tono supplichevole)*
Contessa, perdono. [57]

LA CONTESSA
Più docile io sono,
e dico di sì.

TUTTI
Ah, tutti contenti
saremo così.

Questo giorno di tormenti, [58]
di capricci e di follia,
in contenti e in allegria
solo amor può terminar.
Sposi, amici, al ballo, al gioco!
Alle mine date foco!
Ed al suon di lieta marcia
corriam tutti a festeggiar!

(She tries to kneel, but the Count prevents her.)

COUNT, BASILIO, DON CURZIO, ANTONIO and BARTOLO
Oh Heavens! What do I see?
A delusion, a vision!
That I can't believe.

COUNT *(entreating her)*
My Countess, forgive me. [57]

COUNTESS
I will relent
and say 'Yes'.

ALL
Then let us all
be happy.

This day of torment, [58]
of caprices and folly,
only love can end
in contentment and joy.
Lovers and friends, let's round things off
in dancing and pleasure!
And to the sound of a gay march
let's hasten to the revelry!

Select Discography

For more detailed information of historical and off-the-air recordings of an earlier era, see William Mann, '*Le nozze di Figaro*', *Opera on Record*, ed. Alan Blyth (London: Hutchinson, 1979), p. 70 and C.J. Luten, '*Le nozze di Figaro* (1786)', *The Metropolitan Opera Guide to Recorded Opera*, ed. Paul Gruber (London and New York: Thames and Hudson, 1993), pp. 286–98.

YEAR	CAST COUNT ALMAVIVA COUNTESS ALMAVIVA SUSANNA FIGARO CHERUBINO MARCELLINA DOCTOR BARTOLO DON BASILIO BARBARINA	CONDUCTOR/ORCHESTRA	LABEL
1934–35*	Roy Henderson Aulikki Rautavaara Audrey Mildmay Willi Domgraf-Fassbänder Luise Helletsgruber Constance Willis Norman Allin / Italo Tajo Heddle Nash Winifred Radford	Fritz Busch Glyndebourne Festival	Naxos Historical (omits recitatives and nos. 8, 23–25)

1950*	George London Elisabeth Schwarzkopf Irmgard Seefried Erich Kunz Sena Jurinac Elisabeth Höngen Marjan Rus Erich Majkut Rosl Schwaiger	Herbert von Karajan Vienna Philharmonic	EMI Classics (omits recitatives and nos. 24–25)
1955	Alfred Poell Lisa Della Casa Hilde Gueden Cesare Siepi Suzanne Danco Hilde Rössl-Majdan Fernando Corena Murray Dickie Anny Felbermayer	Erich Kleiber Vienna Philharmonic	Decca Legends
1955*	Franco Calabrese Sena Jurinac Graziella Sciutti Sesto Bruscantini Risë Stevens Monica Sinclair Ian Wallace Hugues Cuénod Jeannette Sinclair	Vittorio Gui Glyndebourne Festival	EMI Classics (omits no. 24)
1956*	Paul Schöffler Sena Jurinac Rita Streich Walter Berry Christa Ludwig Ira Malaniuk Oskar Czerwenka Erich Majkut Rosl Schwaiger	Karl Böhm Vienna Symphony	Philips (omits nos. 24–25)

1959	Eberhard Wächter Elisabeth Schwarzkopf Anna Moffo Giuseppe Taddei Fiorenza Cossotto Dora Gatta Ivo Vinco Renato Ercolani Elisabetta Fusco	Carlo Maria Giulini Philharmonia	EMI Classics (omits nos. 24–25)
1962	Gabriel Bacquier Leyla Gencer Mirella Freni Heinz Blankenburg Edith Mathis Johanna Peters Carlo Cava Hugues Cuénod Maria Zeri	Silvio Varviso Royal Philharmonic	Glyndebourne (live, omits no. 24)
1967	Dietrich Fischer-Dieskau Gundula Janowitz Edith Mathis Hermann Prey Tatiana Troyanos Patricia Johnson Peter Lagger Erwin Wohlfahrt Barbara Vogel	Karl Böhm Deutsche Oper, Berlin	DG
1970	Gabriel Bacquier Elisabeth Söderstrom Reri Grist Geraint Evans Teresa Cahill Annelies Burmeister Michael Langdon Werner Hollweg Margaret Price	Otto Klemperer New Philharmonia	EMI (omits no. 24)

1971	Ingvar Wixell Jessye Norman Mirella Freni Wladimiro Ganzarolli Yvonne Minton Maria Casula Clifford Grant Robert Tear Lillian Watson	Colin Davis Royal Opera House	Philips
1978	Tom Krause Anna Tomowa-Sintow Ileana Cotrubas José van Dam Frederica von Stade Jane Berbié Jules Bastin Heinz Zednik Christine Barbaux	Herbert von Karajan Vienna Philharmonic	Decca
1981	Samuel Ramey Kiri Te Kanawa Lucia Popp Thomas Allen Frederica von Stade Jane Berbié Kurt Moll Robert Tear Yvonne Kenny	Georg Solti London Philharmonic	Decca
1985	Ruggero Raimondi Lucia Popp Barbara Hendricks José van Dam Agnes Baltsa Felicity Palmer Robert Lloyd Aldo Baldin Cathryn Pope	Neville Mariner Academy of St Martin in the Fields	Philips

1987	Jorma Hynninen Margaret Price Kathleen Battle Thomas Allen Ann Murray Mariana Nicolesco Kurt Rydl Alejandro Ramirez Patrizia Pace	Riccardo Muti Vienna Philharmonic	EMI Classics
1987	Richard Stilwell Felicity Lott Gianna Rolandi Claudio Desderi Faith Esham Anne Mason Artur Korn Ugo Benelli Anne Dawson	Bernard Haitink London Philharmonic	EMI Classics
1988	Håkan Hagegård Arleen Augér Barbara Bonney Petteri Salomaa Alicia Nafé Della Jones Carlos Feller Eduardo Giménez Nancy Argenta	Arnold Östman Drottningholm Court Theatre	L'Oiseau-Lyre (on period instruments, including all Prague 1786 and Vienna 1789 variants)
1990	Thomas Hampson Kiri Te Kanawa Dawn Upshaw Ferruccio Furlanetto Anne Sofie von Otter Tatiana Troyanos Paul Plishka Anthony Laciura Heidi Grant	James Levine Metropolitan Opera	DG

1991	Andreas Schmidt Lella Cuberli Joan Rodgers John Tomlinson Cecilia Bartoli Phyllis Pancella Günter von Kannen Graham Clark Hilde Leidland	Daniel Barenboim Berlin Philharmonic	Erato
1993	Rodney Gilfry Hillevi Martinpelto Alison Hagley Bryn Terfel Pamela Helen Stephen Susan McCulloch Carlos Feller Francis Egerton Constanze Backes	John Eliot Gardiner English Baroque Soloists	Archiv (on period instruments and with an idiosyncratic reordering of some numbers in Acts Three and Four)
1993	Thomas Hampson Charlotte Margiono Barbara Bonney Anton Scharinger Petra Lang Ann Murray Kurt Moll Philip Langridge Isabel Rey	Nikolaus Harnoncourt Royal Concertgebouw	Teldec
1994	Bo Skovhus Cheryl Studer Sylvia McNair Lucio Gallo Cecilia Bartoli Anna Caterina Antonacci Ildebrando D'Arcangelo Carlo Allemano Andrea Rost	Claudio Abbado Vienna Philharmonic	DG

1994	Alessandro Corbelli Carol Vaness Nuccia Focile Alastair Miles Suzanne Mentzer Suzanne Murphy Alfonso Antoniozzi Ryland Davies Rebecca Evans	Charles Mackerras	Telarc (including all Prague 1786 and Vienna 1789 variants)
2003	William Dazeley Yvonne Kenny Rebecca Evans Christopher Purves Diana Montague Frances McCafferty Jonathan Veira John Graham-Hall Sarah Tynan	David Parry Philharmonia	Chandos (in English)
2004	Simon Keenlyside Véronique Gens Patricia Ciofi Lorenzo Regazzo Angelika Kirchschlager Marie McLaughlin Antonio Abete Kobie van Rensburg Nuria Rial	René Jacobs Concerto Köln	Harmonia Mundi (on period instruments)
2006	Bo Skovhus Dorothea Röschmann Anna Netrebko Ildebrando D'Arcangelo Christine Schäfer Marie McLaughlin Franz-Josef Selig Patrick Henckens Eva Liebau	Nikolaus Harnoncourt Vienna Philharmonic	DG

* mono

Le nozze di Figaro on DVD, a Selection

For a complete listing, including non-commercial and television films, up to 2004, see Ken Wlaschin, *Encyclopedia of Opera on Screen* (New Haven and London: Yale University Press, 2004), pp. 496–502.

YEAR	CAST	CONDUCTOR	DIRECTOR/COMPANY
	COUNT ALMAVIVA COUNTESS ALMAVIVA SUSANNA FIGARO CHERUBINO MARCELLINA DOCTOR BARTOLO DON BASILIO BARBARINA		
1966*	Ingvar Wixell Claire Watson Reri Grist Walter Berry Edith Mathis Margarethe Bence Zoltán Kélémen David Thaw Diedre Aserford	Karl Böhm Studio film based on Salzburg production	Günther Rennert
1973	Benjamin Luxon Kiri Te Kanawa Ileana Cotrubas Knut Skram Frederica von Stade Nucci Condò Marius Rintzler John Fryatt Janet Perry	John Pritchard Glyndebourne Festival	Peter Hall

1976	Dietrich Fischer-Dieskau Kiri Te Kanawa Mirella Freni Hermann Prey Maria Ewing Heather Begg Paolo Montarsolo John van Kesteren Janet Perry	Karl Böhm Studio film based on Salzburg production	Jean-Pierre Ponnelle
1976+	Uwe Kreyssig Magdalena Falewicz Ursula Reinhart-Kiss Jozsef Dene Ute Trekel-Burckhardt Ruth Schob-Lipka Rudolf Asmus Frank Folker Barbara Sternberger	Géza Oberfrank Komische Oper Berlin	Walter Felsenstein
1980	Gabriel Bacquier Gundula Janowitz Lucia Popp José van Dam Frederica von Stade Jane Berbié Kurt Moll Michel Sénéchal Danièle Perriers	Georg Solti Opéra National de Paris	Giorgio Strehler
1981	Per-Arne Wahlgren Sylvia Lindenstrand Georgine Resick Mikael Samuelson Ann Christine Biel Karin Mang-Habashi Erik Saedén Torbjörn Lillieqvist Birgitta Larsson	Arnold Östman Drottningholm Festival	Göran Järvefelt

1990	James Maddalena Jayne West Jean Ommerlé Sanford Sylvan Susan Larson Sue Ellen Kuzma David Evitts Frank Kelley Lynn Torgove	Craig Smith Studio film based on PepsiCo Summerfare production	Peter Sellars
1991	Ruggero Raimondi Cheryl Studer Marie McLaughlin Lucio Gallo Gabriele Sima Margarita Lilova Rudolf Mazzola Heinz Zednik Yvetta Tannenbergerova	Claudio Abbado Wiener Staatsoper	Jonathan Miller
1993	Rodney Gilfry Hillevi Martinpelto Alison Hagley Bryn Terfel Pamela Helen Stephen Susan McCulloch Carlos Feller Francis Egerton Constanze Backes	John Eliot Gardiner Théâtre du Châtelet	Jean-Louis Thamin
1994	Andreas Schmidt Renée Fleming Alison Hagley Gerald Finley Marie-Ange Todorovitch Wendy Hillhouse Manfred Röhrl Robert Tear Susan Gritton	Bernard Haitink Glyndebourne Festival	Stephen Medcalf

1996	Rodney Gilfry Eva Mei Isabel Rey Carlos Chausson Liliana Nikiteanu Elisabeth von Magnus Robert Holl Volker Vogel Lisa Larsson	Nikolaus Harnoncourt Zurich Opera	Jürgen Flimm
1998	Dwayne Croft Renée Fleming Cecilia Bartoli Bryn Terfel Susanne Mentzer Wendy White Paul Plishka Heinz Zednik Danielle de Niese	James Levine Metropolitan Opera	Jonathan Miller (with Susanna's two 1789 Vienna alternative arias)
1999	Roman Trekel Emily Magee Dorothea Röschmann René Pape Patricia Risley Rosemarie Lang Kwangchul Youn Peter Schreier Yvonne Zeuge	Daniel Barenboim Deutsche Staatsoper	Thomas Langhoff
2004	Pietro Spagnoli Annette Dasch Rosemary Joshua Luca Pisaroni Angelika Kirchschlager Sophie Pondjiclis Antonio Abete Enrico Facini Pauline Courtin	René Jacobs	Jean-Louis Martinoty Théâtre des Champs-Élysées

2006	Peter Mattei Christiane Oelze Heidi Grant Murphy Lorenzo Regazzo Christine Schäfer Helene Schneiderman Roland Bracht Burkhard Ulrich Cassandre Berthon	Sylvain Cambreling Opéra National de Paris	Christoph Marthaler
2006	Bo Skovhus Dorothea Röschmann Anna Netrebko Ildebrando D'Arcangelo Christine Schäfer Marie McLaughlin Franz-Josef Selig Patrick Henckens Eva Liebau	Nikolaus Harnoncourt Salzburg Festival	Claus Guth
2006	Gerald Finley Dorothea Röschmann Miah Persson Erwin Schrott Rinat Shaham Graciela Araya Jonathan Veira Philip Langridge Ana James	Antonio Pappano Royal Opera House	David McVicar

* black and white

\+ in German

Select Bibliography

Abert, Hermann, *W.A. Mozart*, trans. Stewart Spencer (New Haven, CT and London: Yale University Press, 2007)

Angermüller, Rudolph, *Mozart's Operas*, trans. Stewart Spencer (New York, NY: Rizzoli International, 1988)

Beaumarchais, Pierre-Augustin Caron de, *The Figaro Trilogy: The Barber of Seville, The Marriage of Figaro, The Guilty Mother*, trans. David Coward (Oxford: Oxford University Press, 2003)

Bolt, Rodney, *Lorenzo Da Ponte: The Extraordinary Adventures of the Man behind Mozart* (London: Bloomsbury, 2006)

Brophy, Bridget, *Mozart the Dramatist*, revised edn. (London: Libris, 1988)

Cairns, David, *Mozart and His Operas* (London: Allen Lane, 2006)

Carter, Tim, *W.A. Mozart: Le nozze di Figaro* (Cambridge: Cambridge University Press, 1987)

Cox, Cynthia, *The Real Figaro: The Extraordinary Career of Caron de Beaumarchais* (London: Longmans, 1962)

Dent, E.J., *Mozart's Operas: A Critical Study*, 2nd edn. (Oxford: Oxford University Press, 1947)

Einstein, Alfred, *Mozart, His Character, His Work*, trans. Arthur Mendel and Nathan Broder (London: Cassell, 1946)

Eisen, Cliff and Keefe, Simon P. (eds.), *The Cambridge Mozart Encyclopedia* (Cambridge: Cambridge University Press, 2006)

Eisen, Cliff (ed.), *Mozart: A Life in Letters*, trans. Stewart Spencer (London: Penguin, 2006)

Grendel, Frédéric, *Beaumarchais: The Man Who Was Figaro*, trans. Roger Graves (London: Macdonald and Jane's, 1977)

Gutman, Robert W., *Mozart: A Cultural Biography* (New York, NY: Harcourt Brace & Co., 1999)

Heartz, Daniel, *Mozart's Operas* (Berkeley, CA: University of California Press, 1990)

Holden, Anthony, *The Man Who Wrote Mozart: The Extraordinary Life of Lorenzo Da Ponte* (London: Weidenfeld & Nicolson, 2006)

Hunter, Mary, *Mozart's Operas: A Companion* (New Haven, CT and London: Yale University Press, 2008)

Keefe, Simon P. (ed.), *The Cambridge Companion to Mozart* (Cambridge: Cambridge University Press, 2003)

Kerman, Joseph, *Opera as Drama* (New York, NY: Alfred Knopf, 1956, rev. 2005)

Landon, H.C. Robbins, *Mozart, the Golden Years 1781–1791* (London: Thames & Hudson, 1989)

Landon, H.C. Robbins (ed.), *The Mozart Compendium* (London: Thames & Hudson, 1990)

Landon, H.C. Robbins and Donald Mitchell (eds.), *The Mozart Companion* (London: Rockliff, 1956)

Mann, William, *The Operas of Mozart* (London: Cassell, 1977)

Moberly, R.B., *Three Mozart Operas* (London: Dodd Mead, 1967)

Rushton, Julian (ed.), *The New Grove Guide to Mozart and His Operas* (Oxford: Oxford University Press, 2007)

Sadie, Stanley (ed.), *Wolfgang Amadè Mozart* (Oxford: Clarendon Press, 1996)

Steptoe, Andrew, *The Mozart–Da Ponte Operas* (Oxford: Clarendon, 1988)

Till, Nicholas, *Mozart and the Enlightenment: Truth, Virtue and Beauty in Mozart's Operas* (London: Faber and Faber, 1992)

Mozart Websites

In English or with an English-language option*

Apropos Mozart	www.aproposmozart.com
Associazione Mozart Italia	www.mozartitalia.org
Bärenreiter Mozart Portal	www.mozart-portal.de
Mozart's Musical Diary (British Library Online Gallery)	www.bl.uk/onlinegallery/ttp/ttpbooks.html
International Mozart Foundation	www.mozarteum.at
The Mozart Forum	www.mozartforum.com
The Mozart Project	www.mozartproject.org
Neue Mozart-Ausgabe Online	www.nma.at
OperaGlass Mozart	opera.stanford.edu/Mozart
Salzburg Festival	www.salzburgfestival.com

* The information on this page is liable to change, but all links were valid at the time of publication in 2011.

Note on the Contributors

Basil Deane was a musicologist, academic and arts administrator. Among the positions he held was Professor of Music at the Barber Institute of Fine Arts at the University of Birmingham. He died in 2006.

George Hall writes widely on classical music and especially opera, including for the *Guardian*, *Opera*, *Opera News* and *BBC Music Magazine*.

Max Loppert was Chief Music and Opera Critic of the London *Financial Times* from 1980 to 1996. Since 2000 he has lived in north-east Italy, from where he reviews performances for *Opera* while working on his large-scale study of the operas of Gluck.

Stephen Oliver was a prolific composer whose works included operas, music theatre, orchestral and chamber music, as well as much incidental music for stage and screen. His final opera, *Timon of Athens*, was staged by ENO in 1992. He died the following year, aged forty-two.

Julian Rushton, Emeritus Professor of Music at the University of Leeds, has published extensively on Mozart, including *The New Grove Guide to Mozart's Operas* and the Cambridge Opera Handbook on *Idomeneo*. He also contributed to the Overture Opera Guide to *Idomeneo*.

David Syrus is Head of Music at Covent Garden. He joined the company in 1971 as a répétiteur and has gone on to conduct over fifty performances of Mozart operas with the Royal Opera. As a continuo player he has worked both there and in Salzburg, Paris, Munich, Barcelona and Frankfurt.

John Wells was an author, translator and performer. He was one of the original contributors to *Private Eye*. His stage work includes a revised version of the text of *Candide* with Leonard Bernstein. He died in 1998.

Acknowledgements

We would like to thank John Allison of *Opera* magazine, Charles Johnston, Julian Rushton and Mike Ashman for their assistance and advice in the preparation of this guide.